THE DEMOCRATIC VISTA

THE DEMOCRATIC VISTA
A Dialogue on Life and Letters
in Contemporary America

by Richard Chase

Doubleday Anchor Books
Doubleday & Company, Inc., Garden City, New York
1958

TYPOGRAPHY BY EDWARD GOREY

Library of Congress Catalog Card Number 58–7351

ACKNOWLEDGMENTS

Considerable portions of this book first appeared in the form of essays and review articles. These were as follows: "Walt Whitman as American Spokesman," *Commentary* (March, 1955); "Is There a Middle Way in Culture?", *Commentary* (July, 1955); "Middlebrow England," *Commentary* (September, 1956); "Radicalism in the American Novel," *Commentary* (January, 1957); "Radicalism Today: A Dialogue," *Partisan Review* (Winter, 1957); "Neo-Conservatism and American Literature," *Commentary* (March, 1957); "Heresy and Modern Culture," *Dissent* (Spring, 1957); "The Fate of the Avant-Garde," *Partisan Review* (Summer, 1957).

In writing this book I have been conscious of a debt to many authors and to many friends—a debt I cannot undertake to acknowledge here. I should mention, however, the contributors to the "Young Generation" series of articles that appeared in the *New Leader* while I was writing my book, especially Norman Podhoretz, Robert Lekachman, Daniel Bell, and Anatole Shub. On two or three occasions when my characters called Ralph and George manage to talk perceptively, they are using the words of my friend and correspondent, R. W. Flint. In the "Saturday Morning" section certain paragraphs have been taken from my earlier book, *The American Novel and Its Tradition* (Anchor, 1957).

Doubleday would like to thank the following publishers for their kind permission to reprint passages in *The Democratic Vista*.

America's Coming of Age, by Van Wyck Brooks, E. P. Dutton and Company, Inc., New York.

Cape Ann and *Salvages*, by T. S. Eliot, Harcourt, Brace and Company, Inc., New York, and Faber and Faber Ltd., London.

The Chrysanthemum and the Sword, by Ruth Benedict, Houghton Mifflin Company, Boston.

The Education of Henry Adams, Chapter I, by Henry Adams, Houghton Mifflin Company, Boston.

Four Quartets, by T. S. Eliot (copyright, 1943, by T. S. Eliot), Harcourt, Brace and Company, Inc., New York, and Faber and Faber Ltd., London.

The Hero with a Thousand Faces, by Joseph Campbell, Bollingen Series XVII, Pantheon Books, Inc., New York.

Literary History of the United States, by Robert E. Spiller and others, The Macmillan Company, New York.

Mont-Saint-Michel and Chartres, by Henry Adams, Houghton Mifflin Company, Boston.

A Piece of My Mind, by Edmund Wilson, Farrar, Straus and Cudahy, Inc., New York.

Sailing to Byzantium, by William Butler Yeats, The Macmillan Company, New York.

That Uncertain Feeling, by Kingsley Amis, Harcourt, Brace and Company, Inc., New York.

The White Goddess, by Robert Graves, by permission of Robert Graves, A. P. Watt and Sons, London.

An article by Daniel Bell in *The New Leader*, The New Leader, New York.

INTRODUCTORY NOTE

The characters in the ensuing dialogue disagree with each other a good deal in their talk about current psychological, moral, political, sexual, literary, and other matters. And in order to give a clear idea of themselves they speak, a little artificially, as members of different generations. Yet they all illustrate different facets of the "interim" or cold-war state of mind which has typified the last ten or fifteen years of American life.

To the character called Ralph, his friend George's argument that this is not an interim period in the development of American culture but quite possibly a final maturing and success seems merely another example of interim thinking. Ralph regards the "success" of our civilization as illusory and believes that, despite our material advance, the general tone of the life we have been living—in the quality of its thought and of its moral and aesthetic expression—leaves much to be desired. The last decade seems to him a time of denial, of retreat, of short-range vistas and purblind projects. He thinks of it as at best a time of revision and retrenchment that quite properly followed the great burst of creative and critical activity that took place in this country in the forty years, or a little less, after 1912. The interim years seem to him to have undeniable virtues of the minor order, virtues of critical acumen and wisdom in the ways of life, but to be only a period of preparation for a new liberation and flowering of culture. Not that he, or any of the other characters, knows when this will happen or what form it will take. But they spend some time trying to discern the future, mostly by commenting on the present and the past. The persons of the dialogue, I should add, are all imaginary, although some of them are composites of people I have known. Ralph, however, usually speaks for the author.

The dialogue is very far from pretending to include every facet of contemporary thought. For example, although religion is talked about, there is no person of theological convictions in the piece, and no existentialist. Neither of these, as such, would have had a great deal to say to the point—the point being a radical reconsideration of American culture, particularly but by no means exclusively its political and literary aspects.

R. C.

THE DEMOCRATIC VISTA

PERSONS OF THE DIALOGUE

RALPH HEADSTRONG, a professor, middle-aging.

DOROTHY HEADSTRONG, housewife and erstwhile social worker.

GEORGE MIDDLEBY, solid citizen of the new generation.

NANCY MIDDLEBY, his wife.

MAGGIE MOTIVE, a glamorous amateur and woman of projects, out of the gay past.

RINALDO SCHULTZ, optimist, engineer, and newly naturalized American.

DARLENE, baby-sitter.

CHILDREN, in quantity.

Friday Evening:

The Life of the Mind, *en Famille*

The scene is the kitchen of the summer place where the Headstrongs—Ralph, Dorothy, and four children—have spent the latter part of the season. It is now September and the evening has come early. The dinner has been a large one, the visiting George and Nancy Middleby having added, with their two children, four persons to the seven regular inhabitants of the house —for there is also Darlene, the teen-age baby-sitter. At the moment everyone except Ralph and George is upstairs, where the children are being gradually put to bed. Ralph is finishing the dishwashing—a ritual which he silently performs with his usual mixture of dull resentment and forced exhilaration, while George bumbles abstractedly about the unfamiliar kitchen, now and then drying a glass. As they finish up, George lights a cigarette and steps outside. Ralph pauses to toss upstairs the diaper Dorothy has shouted for, deftly catches the wet one tossed down in return, drops it in the diaper pail, swats a fly, throws out the cat, wraps up the garbage, and joins George outside.

They have been trying to talk before, but nothing much could get said in the general hubbub. Ralph at one point had got so far as to say, rather awkwardly, "The life of ideas, the life of the mind, though somewhat improbable, still seems to be possible under modern conditions as we know them. . . ." But at that moment the cat scratched Bobby and Bobby's wails drowned out all else. Now Ralph suggests a twilight stroll.

Although Nancy Middleby is thirty and Dorothy Headstrong is forty-one, they became fast friends a number of years ago while working in the same Family Welfare Agency in New York. But this is the first time their husbands have talked at any length. There is no doubt that they bring to each other a ready supply of good will. Ralph is already pleased with George's easy friendliness and air of bonhomie, as well as the impression he gives of being established by temperament, rather than by his actual worldly position, in the social life of man. George in turn is much taken with Ralph, whom he still thinks of as Professor Headstrong, although he will soon be calling him by his first name. Clearly the Professor is a novel character.

The path they take leads down a long, gentle slope through the scrub oak, wild roses, bayberry, and blueberry bushes toward the massive jumble of granite on which the Atlantic breaks before them. As they look back over the dull green expanse they have already crossed, the gray clapboard house with its steeply pitched roof and moderate gingerbread décor looms up among its locust and hickory trees against the western sky. The voices of children being cajoled and wheedled to bed can still be heard from the second story of the house. But it is the prospect before them that George and Ralph survey as they talk—the tremendous geometrical chaos of boulders and ledges and beyond these a trawler and a lobster boat silently making for the Annisquam River. To the north the flat rays of the sun still light hilltops along the New Hampshire coast and a dark haze begins to appear on the horizon of the seascape to the east and northeast.

RALPH: I'm glad you waited until September to visit

us. The Massachusetts coast is at its most beautiful now, and will be for the next six weeks. It is clear and cool at this time of year, barring northeasters, and most of the summer people have left. The shadows are dark and the light is brilliant. This appeals both to my simple aesthetic requirements and to my misanthropy.

GEORGE: It is good of you to have me and my brood up here. The apartment in Cambridge grew very confining; it's great to have a change. But are you really a misanthropist?

RALPH: It is a mood I like to indulge. I get a gloomy pleasure, for example, out of haunting summer resorts and beaches in the winter. Look up the coast to Newburyport, where you can just now catch the last glint of light on the water tower, and try to imagine what it was like in these parts when there were fewer people —one hundred, two hundred, or three hundred years ago.

GEORGE: I should imagine these rocks and the surf that breaks on them haven't changed much. The vegetation hereabouts has a slumbrous, eternal look.

RALPH: It's easy to feel here what people felt for the first time in its full force in the nineteenth century —the apparent anomalousness of human life in the universe.

GEORGE: The universe as such doesn't bother me— I mean, I am not aware of it. It bores me and I am content with the happy delusion that *it* is anomalous, except as it contributes to the conditions of life which I wish to make for myself. So you see, I am not worried about whether man and his mind are alien in the universe. What really concerns me is the various forms of social anomaly or alienation that confront us. Being a professor certainly puts one in an ambiguous position in the social order. People regard professors with a strange ambivalence, not knowing whether to admire or despise them and so doing both—at least that is what I've been thinking more and more during the summer session of the graduate school.

RALPH: There are many questions I would like to talk over with you. For example, aren't you perhaps a little too sensitive about social anomaly? To offer a rash generalization in unsatisfactory terms, I think there is truth in the familiar charge that your generation is sadly conservative, moralistic, "other-directed," and earth-bound—or rather, I should say, community-bound. It seems to me that young people have lost the courage to fail and are too ready to settle for a half success. I can't help admiring the older puritan type who was prepared to fail spectacularly and, as it were, on purpose, in pursuit of triumph. He assumed that in order to soar high, he had to be ready to fall ignominiously. It seems that people nowadays are afraid to be alone, as notable failure or notable success makes one alone. At the same time, I perceive in you a sense of social fact and an ability to rest solidly in the concrete moment of emotion that may well put my abstractions to the test. Anyway, I'd like to hear your thoughts on such matters as the continuing possibility of the life of the mind in our contemporary America. Will it be possible to keep alive, in an atmosphere of growing conformity, a fruitful versatility of taste and opinion, or are all forms of expression and feeling, above the level of the mass media, being boiled down into a sort of middlebrow mush where all distinctions are lost? How are we to reconcile the American imagination as we find it in our literature—on the whole a literature of extremity, of brilliant fragments, of melodrama, humor, pastoral idyl, and romance—with the mild, routine life of the new suburban America? Do the inherited attitudes of our life and experience sanction in any way the political and cultural conservatism of the Eisenhower Age? Is there a possibility (supposing it to be desirable) of keeping alive the radical, avant-garde views on which I was brought up in the 1930's, so that they will not die out in the present decade and will therefore be ready for a future resurgence of creative activity? The history of America has been the history of a continuing revolt. Will the revolt continue, or has America finally grown old and complacent and content to settle its accounts and retire on its memories? Or is there perhaps already a visible resurgence?

GEORGE: Very large and difficult questions. . . .

RALPH: Which we surely don't have to settle tonight. Let's start with a more immediate matter. Your generation of students, teachers, writers, artists, and professional people—and to a considerable extent mine too—has gone in for children and the hazards and comforts of family life. The generation of the 1920's would have regarded this as a personal disaster, as far as the free creative life or even the academic life was concerned. Surely, they were wrong about that. But in saddling ourselves with children and a position in society we have saddled ourselves with a lot of new problems. One can hardly sleep with one's wife without generating, as it were, a perplexing ideology of the new life in America. Do you suppose it was better in the twenties?

GEORGE: I doubt it. All the gay lovers of the twenties had was high-tension, quick-triggered encounters. Me for the quiet, neatly lawned street and the rumpled suburban bed. But the questions you have just raised interest me deeply—along with several others I can think of—and I'll be disappointed if we don't get a chance to thrash them out. Also I want you to tell me sometime this week end why I should not give up my plans to be a teacher and go into the insurance business. I have been offered a very attractive job in insurance and I expect to accept. Should I consider myself a renegade because I want to make the equivalent of a full professor's salary in three years instead of twenty-five? This is one of many questions that occur to me. However, for the moment, I am content with the scenery. I can even share your misanthropy, although such is not my nature.

RALPH: On your left there, a hawk is sailing from the dead top of the oak by the granite quarry. Doesn't that bring the savage world back to you? It puts me in mind of Robinson Jeffers, whose response to the totally populated, paved, and urbanized America of the future is a cry of utopian despair:

> The cities gone down, the people fewer and the
>   hawks more numerous,
> The rivers mouth to source pure; when the two-
>   footed
> Mammal, being someways one of the nobler ani-
>   mals, regains
> The dignity of room, the value of rareness.

GEORGE: Sounds like a combination of Nietzsche and a ferocious and embattled frontiersman. It is very moving, and I respond to it. Still, I stumble over that "two-footed mammal" business—the pessimism implied by that phrase seems to be merely a cheap bit of "philosophy," lacking the authentic conviction of the rest. I trust his feeling about hawks but not about people.

RALPH: You are right. Jeffers is not really a favorite of mine, yet the clang of the offshore bell, the darkening colors of the sea, the lost human voice of the seagulls that you can hear when they hover close over you —all this conduces to a romantic loneliness. But if one is going in for apocalyptic feelings, I suppose T. S. Eliot's theological tone is more humane. He must have

stood right here when the poem he calls "Cape Ann"
came to him:

> . . . resign this land at the end, resign it
> To its true owner, the tough one, the seagull.

Jeffers' pessimism is more typically American than
Eliot's. But for him, as for all our "naturalistic" writers,
pessimism—as you suggest—is too much an act of the
intellect. It is too abstract, willful, and crude both in
its emotional and intellectual component. Whitman is
surely a greater poet than Jeffers, who is an inverted
Whitman. In Jeffers, pessimism and misanthropy and
the belief in Fate or Necessity stamp out all subtlety,
wit, and versatility. Whitman's optimism and good-
fellowship, his belief in free will and the autonomous,
self-justifying Self often make him vague and bathetic,
but they do not spoil his wit and his surprising vital
diversity.

GEORGE: I seem to be a benighted soul, Professor. I
can't bring myself to admire or understand Whitman
—an odd situation for anyone who has thought seriously of teaching American literature, or for anyone
who claims to like and hopes to understand the American writers. To be quite frank, American literature
makes me uneasy and unhappy. It seems to mirror so
few of the moral and aesthetic qualities I admire. And
despite my patriotic impulses and my fascination with
the subject, I always fall back on English literature because there I find represented in greater richness the
kinds of human experience I understand. Outside of
the tradition of Henry James and Howells, these kinds
of experience seem to me to be ignored or cryptically
distorted by the American writers.

Actually, it is not only *American* literature that
leaves me dissatisfied. Literature itself, as something
to be taught and discussed year after year, literature

as a way of life for a person who does not create it
seems less and less attractive to me. Literary Americans are *too* literary—when they see a hawk, if you'll
pardon me for saying so, they think not of a hawk but
of something a poet said about hawks. When I was
studying at Cambridge University after the war, it
used to strike me how much more gracefully and less
grimly the Europeans wear their literature.

RALPH: I know what you mean. But . . . it is getting
dark. Shall we go back to the house? I will show you
our quarry tomorrow. We might have walked back by
the quarry path, but it is already too dark for you to
get the full effect of the spectacle. The local people
show a sound sense of poetic language in calling it "the
pit"—a resonant word out of the rocky Calvinistic soul
of Massachusetts. The pit, from which half the paving
stones of Boston were quarried, by Finnish labor imported for the purpose, has long been abandoned and
nature has reclaimed it by filling it with spring and
rain water. (*A pause.*) If you listen sharp you will hear
the first notes of the whippoorwill; it is one of the earliest sounds I remember. But I am afraid you are not
a nature lover. If so, isn't that a bit anomalous in one
who thinks so highly of English literature?

GEORGE: I suppose it is. As I say, I have nothing
against nature. I can take it or leave it. I truly respond
to this beautiful place. I sense what Eliot meant in
"The Dry Salvages": "The salt is on the briar rose,"
and what is that about the sea? Yes, it comes back:

The sea is the land's edge also, the granite
Into which it reaches, the beaches where it tosses
Its hints of earlier and other creation.

But you are right, I don't really feel comfortable in
natural surroundings. It always occurs to me when I
am in nature's midst that if one is going to be sur-

rounded by objects, they may as well be human artifacts. To my taste, nature is too dispersed, redundant,
open, and fortuitous. It lacks order, selectivity, and
moral significance—especially this gaunt and rugged
coast. But I don't wish to sound ungrateful; I have told
you how happy we are to be here.

RALPH: Well, the house seems quiet. The lights are
on in the living room. Let us surround ourselves with
human artifacts. If the girls are through gossiping, perhaps they will talk to us.

*The living room is long and low, a combination of
summer cottage style of the older sort with a substan-
tial* décor *of wood-paneling on the walls; there is one
oak beam in the ceiling. Besides the fireplace and the
array of miscellaneous furniture, there are a distinguished walnut highboy and a number of book shelves,
one containing a respectable library of works in Greek
and Latin. There is also a small organ with one row of
keys, and pedals to supply the air pressure; a hymnal
is on the music stand. A large number of objects are
seen about the room—a sword, some coats of arms, several statuettes, a Turkish water pipe, a candle snuffer,
some glass fish-net floats, a plaque showing Adam and
Eve in a rustic, Renoiresque style. On the chairs and
floor are some children's things—a sneaker, a pair of
bathing trunks, a sweater.*

NANCY: George, come and sit here, with me. Don't
you love this room? Dorothy says the style is Fitzpat-
rick-Adamant.

DOROTHY: The place was built and the *objets d'art*
assembled by Fitzpatrick, a well-to-do textile manu-
facturer who retired in order to dabble in art and ideas.
His taste seems to have been eclectic, to say the least.
During the thirties there was apparently a summer sa-

lon of bohemians here: in morals, free; in art, eclectic-avant-garde; in politics, socialist to Stalinist. The Adamants, Bob and his mother (through whose generosity we are here) have got rid of a lot of the junk left by the departed Fitzpatrick, including a crumbling gazebo that used to extend from the side porch. They have kept the better furnishings and art works and added some of their own. It is said that Dos Passos slept here.

GEORGE: It looks fine. The spirit of the place is no longer avant-garde—I mean, what I like about it is that it has all the comforts of home and some of the restful atmosphere of a museum. Or anyway, it would if the children would go to sleep.

Upstairs can be heard the sounds of subdued chatter, with occasional shrieks from Bobby and Herman, who are trying to adjust themselves to being in the same bed. The tinny sound of little Nat's electric victrola ($8.00 plus 23 cereal box tops) can be heard; Nat is lulled to sleep nightly by Elvis Presley singing "All Shook Up."

GEORGE (*musingly*): Ah, it puts me in a mood to recite Longfellow:

> Between the dark and the daylight,
>   When the night is beginning to lower,
> Comes a pause in the day's occupations,
>   That is known as the Children's Hour.

> I hear in the chamber above me
>   The patter of little feet,
> The sound of a door that is opened,
>   And voices soft and sweet.

> From my study I see in the lamplight,
>   Descending the broad hall stair,

Grave Alice and laughing Allegra,
And Edith with golden hair.

RALPH: The son of a bitch.

DOROTHY: Ralph!

RALPH: I'm going to compose an up-to-date poem called "The Children's Twenty-Four Hours."

DOROTHY: Oh, come now. It isn't as bad as all that. You're just jealous. Actually you are a true modern, but you imagine that you would like to have a long white beard, live in a Georgian house, play the heavy Victorian father, write inferior verse, and make the populace bow to you in the streets.

RALPH: I would, for a fact.

DOROTHY: Nonsense. You wouldn't like it, even though playing the privileged patriarch might soothe your wounded ego a bit. And I certainly wouldn't like to be Mrs. Longfellow.

RALPH: You'd have several servants, and I wouldn't have to wash dishes.

GEORGE: I certainly share some of Ralph's sentiments, although I perceive that for dialectical purposes his remarks are somewhat facetious. I'm impatient with self-pitying husbands, but in a way it's not surprising that there are so many of them around. You ladies have been living for generations now with the problems arising from the changes of your status in the home and the world at large. But history has caught up with the fathers of families suddenly, so that for the first time we find ourselves doing a share of all those things the vanishing servant class once did—dishwashing, baby-sitting, shopping, and so on. The male is usually distinguished from the female by his capacity to concentrate his creative energies to one purpose, his life-work. But now he often has to accommodate himself to several careers, including domestic responsibilities his father wouldn't have thought of undertaking. Then, there are the lugubrious statistics, the early deaths and the inadequate income for the widow and children. Naturally, the adjustment all this implies cannot be accomplished without neurotic symptoms, particularly by a man who has any sort of ego.

NANCY: I'm not surprised that you embattled fathers enjoy fantasies of yourselves as the stern and aloof patriarch, or as Don Juan. And I think you should have your innings; after all, women have been indulging in escapist fantasies ever since Emma Bovary, in fact ever since Eve. And I'm not surprised that George should be taken aback when I refer to him as "you and the other children"—which I've done by mistake on at least two occasions. But what pleases me is that the father has been made a real part of the modern family. His relations with children and wife may not be all pleasant, but they are real and, in many cases, continuous. I don't think we will have the stricken and bereaved children that the old-fashioned family turned out. The modern family may be full of hate as well as of love, but the human contact is there—or would be if only there were fewer divorces.

DOROTHY: I think my dear Ralph is rather preposterously romantic, as well as just plain mistaken, about the deterioration of the father image. Still, I can sympathize with his feelings.

RALPH: It is rather depressing to have the feeling, as I do sometimes, that to my children I am just another child, the only difference being that I am bigger, physically stronger, and always have money in my pocket.

GEORGE: I'll bet I speak for Dorothy when I say that you are wrong about that, or at any rate, about its implications. True, one of the phenomena of the time is the child-husband, just as the child-wife was a phenomenon of the older culture. Pop is one of the kids all right. But that has its pleasant and appealing side too. I look forward to the growing companionship with my children.

RALPH: Well, I admit that in what I have said I have been responding more to a public archetype than to the reality. But I do despise the grinning, boyish father image, created in the popular mind by the ad-men of our maudlin era of "other-direction" and rest-less consumption. The Amiable Consumer makes me long for the Nietzschean Superman, for the whip, the scourge, for the desert vigil—except, that is, when I am amiably consuming.

At the open window, a face becomes suddenly visible in the light of the table lamp—a woman's face, broadly lipsticked and smiling, and festivally wreathed in foliage.

NANCY (*blurting it out*): Heavens! It's the Medusa!

DOROTHY: Maggie! Come on in and sit down.

MAGGIE: No thank you. I was just taking a stroll and now I must get home. Besides you are probably having one of the tiresome discussions you young people go in for nowadays. I only want to invite you all over for a drink tomorrow afternoon. These would be the friends you said were coming?

DOROTHY: Nancy and George Middleby—Maggie Motive.

RALPH: Our oracle, our free spirit, our——

MAGGIE: Peeping Tom. I will see you tomorrow. The hemlock needles are trickling down my neck. Good night all. (*She disappears.*)

RALPH: I was about to say that Maggie is our Spirit of the Twenties, but she is a little sensitive about her age. Actually, she is only a few years older than I, but her attitudes were first formed in the 1920's, as mine and Dorothy's were in the thirties, and the Middlebys' in the forties. We have the makings of an inter-generational jamboree.

NANCY: Oddly enough, the recent revivals of the twenties, in musical comedies, TV skits, and so on, have made me feel that I am more akin to that decade than to the thirties. Not that I'm a particularly giddy character, or a flapper.

GEORGE: I think that's natural. In the fifties people look for fulfillment in the personal life, as they did in the twenties. Ideological problems and the unfolding of history are as perplexing now as they were in the 1930's, but for most people they don't bear directly on day-to-day experience. In the twenties, the goal of most people, aside from getting rich quick, was, as someone says, to "give a clear shape to the merely personal life." People feel this in the fifties, although in a different way. A character in one of Kingsley Amis' novels suggests the sameness and the difference when he reflects that nowadays "it wasn't so much doing what you wanted to do that was important . . . as wanting to do what you did." I agree with Nancy. "Our generation" sees the 1920's more clearly than it sees the Depression period; we respond, or would like to respond, to its currents of emotion. We would like to take from that gay and doomed decade some of its licentiousness and iconoclastic wit, as well as its ideal of the personal life. Yet the situation demands, of course, a profound change in what is expected of the personal life. It is no longer a matter of self-fulfillment through uninhibited behavior or through romantic gestures or heroic quests or sublime tragicomic collapses and assertions.

RALPH: It is a matter of "other-directedness," community spirit, and conformity?

NANCY: Partly that. But as for myself, these are not ideals. They are means toward the end of wanting to do what you do. What you do, if you are anything like the Middlebys, is try to bring up children on an income which nominally increases slowly but steadily decreases in purchasing power. What you do, is struggle to achieve social and economic status. In the attempt to make life personally bearable and significant for yourself and your children, you don't have the time or energy to worry about whether you are turning into a faceless exurbanite or a conformist. You take what comfort you can in the community feeling, in the feeling that others are in the same boat.

I don't see, by the way, how one can oppose conformity as such, as the would-be radicals seem to do. It is always a question of what is being conformed to and why. After all, civilization itself is impossible without certain kinds of conformity. One of the things I conform to is the high standard of female efficiency I see in the suburbs. If my sense of "belonging" helps me to bring up my family, balance the budget, keep myself attractive to my husband, and impress upon my children that TV, suburban life, and group activity are not the sum total of the world's culture, I don't apologize for conforming, or for lacking the desperate gaiety of the twenties or the passionate commitments of the thirties. There was so much tension and instability in those decades. What I want to do is relax, not into mediocrity, if I can help it, but into the natural conditions of my being as a social animal.

DOROTHY: What struck me when I first became aware of a new generation not quite my own was how little the old cultural idols meant to it. It's a long way from the summer labor school where I used to teach at the end of the 1930's, with its earnest devotion to world revolt and reform, to the suburbs. But I've made the grade after my fashion and I am not surprised that our experience of status-seeking, bill-paying, diaper-changing, and dishwashing should have finally forced me to feel what Nancy has come more naturally and easily to feel.

GEORGE: It's not surprising that there has been a considerable scaling down of intellectual ambition. I think personally I've done justice to the literary gods of the first four decades of the century—to Henry James, Shaw, T. S. Eliot, Virginia Woolf, Joyce, Pound, W. H. Auden. At the same time I admit that to me it seems that the greatest writers of the first half of the twentieth century lived in a high, tense world of strenuous and difficult metaphysics, moral doctrine, political ideology, and religious feeling which it is no longer possible to share. They seem to have striven for an impossibly high ideal of artistic craftsmanship and for an expressive form which was too dependent on abstractions, universals, myths, and symbols. I want to bring literature and ideas back into touch with life as I know it, back to the personal life. The fact that the personal life is led in a community or a suburb, that it is organized and is a form of group activity, seems to me neither good nor bad, since it is obviously inevitable.

RALPH: La-de-da. But of course you are right, in a way.

GEORGE: Well, Ralph, you, having four children, know how impossible it is to take the cultural high-road, the primrose path of the bourgeois intellectual who flourished, say, from 1910 to 1940. He was typically urbanite (at least in spirit) and if he was married, he and his wife had decided from the beginning that they would have no children. You have seen, as I have, how little conducive to the free intelligence and the pursuit of culture is the university life that young people now lead, before they ever get to the suburban housing development. There is a new proletariat now —the impoverished graduate students, teachers, laboratory technicians, and librarians who live in their cramped apartments, crowded shacks, and trailers in the vicinity of our large universities.

The status-seeking inhabitants of these sprawling communities are brought much more immediately into contact with the facts of life than those who formed their ideas in the twenties and thirties are likely to have been. Books by the great thinkers who meant so much to an earlier generation—Marx, Nietzsche, Freud —these may be found in the orange-crate bookcases in the flimsy shacks and Quonset huts, along with volumes by the difficult modern poets and novelists. Picasso and Klee may be seen on the dingy walls, and there are records by Bach and Mozart, along with some jazz and folk songs. But much more real and pressing than the life of ideas and of art is the spectacle of life as it is being actually led—with its hard work, its insecurity, its abnegation, its nervous fatigue, with its domestic duties and the ever-present children, whom their parents must perpetually consider, even when engaging in the rather grubby sexual infidelities that make one of the few sources of diversion. Such a life leaves little enough energy to run after the intellectual gods of an earlier generation, and these were gods, it must be admitted, who required of their votaries a strenuous worship.

RALPH: Still, can't we bourgeois family men be free in the life of the mind—we Miltons, Melvilles, and Manns? Must the damp diaper suffuse with its urgent reality even the most soaring ideas, the most fervently pure of commitments?

NANCY: There are other real things in the world beside damp diapers. Many people my age seem to have a new sense of social reality, for example, and of the limitation of human aspiration. Measured against reality, the soaring ideas and pure commitments you speak of seem rather quixotic. Certainly the great ideas and unexamined aspirations of the twenties and thirties led many people into error, grief, and disillusionment. Isn't it possible to learn by experience?

GEORGE: Of course it is. Our moralizing elders have been telling us for years of the immense human cost of the discontinuity of American civilization. It is ridiculous, they say, that every generation should be a totally new thing in the world, with no sense of what went before. And now that a new generation has appeared, the chief distinguishing mark of which is that it *has* learned by experience, it is chided by its elders for being tame and dull and old before its time. What do they want us to do—make the same old mistakes all over again, just to prove that our heart is in the right place?

DOROTHY: I can't help thinking that a colorful gesture of some sort every now and then might make your generation a bit more picturesque.

NANCY: Do you refer to the nude midnight swim?

DOROTHY: Well, the midnight swim was once a cultural episode, a gesture of release and pleasure. I suspect that now it is indulged in only by middle-aged people and by high school students who do it as a matter of course and are already bored with it. But you will admit, won't you, that underneath the mature self-assurance of your generation there lurks a restlessness?

NANCY: I think it's pretty much confined to the intellectuals.

GEORGE: They feel the unhappiness and the guilt of a generation which has not defined itself as clearly as did their predecessors and which, to the extent that it *has* defined itself has tended to do so negatively, by what it has given up. And despite the obvious advantages of learning from experience, there is a certain unhappiness in living on an unearned income, in living on a moral capital amassed for us by our elders. Rather than winning wisdom in pain and trouble, we have been bequeathed wisdom.

RALPH: As a rule I'm against "wisdom"—although it is certainly one of the key words of the time. I prefer skill, improvisation, an eye for the hard fact, a taste for irony and abstraction. I don't know why people like wisdom so much; it is a soggy, gloomy, cryptic, moralistic habit of mind. I've noticed that most students nowadays come to literature with the sole idea of getting wisdom out of it. There are no midnight swims for the wise. They would be full of social aplomb but afraid of getting their bottoms mossy. Have you any other cultural symbols, Dorothy?

DOROTHY: Yes, from the movies. For the 1920's Clara Bow is inevitable—the frivolous, sentimental, dynamic flapper. In fact the It girl. For the present day I nominate Elizabeth Taylor, whom the slick magazines describe as "the girl who grew up too soon." They show us her sad, wistful, little-girl's face, and enumerate her several husbands. She is youth looking at itself and being dismayed by the fact that it is already spiritually old without ever having been young.

RALPH: Clara Bow had It, whereas Elizabeth Taylor has had it—is that what you mean?

DOROTHY (paying no attention): At fifteen, American girls know what I didn't know until I was twenty-one and much that my mother never knew. Yet their weary maturity has come to them as a part of the convention of modern living. They did not have to earn it.

NANCY: And the thirties?

DOROTHY: Carole Lombard. She made life brighter in those years, before the tragic airplane crash. She was not a flapper, nor a little girl too soon grown up. She

had something of the gaiety and recklessness of the
flapper, but she was also the ordinary, companionable
girl who lives down the street. In one movie she is
called (before she marries Robert Montgomery) Annie
Krausheimer. She played mostly in sophisticated comedies. It is true that in these movies nobody starved
or had to sell apples, but under the frivolous surface
there was a sadness and a concern for human suffering.
She knew much more about the way people live and
the trials they go through than the flapper knew. Not
that she ever played the part of a social worker, but she
had a very effective way of wrinkling her brow that
endeared her to people who were worried over sag-
ging bank accounts and the general precariousness of
the age. Despite her vitality and her solid bourgeois
constitution, she was always subject to sudden rever-
sals of fortune. But she always bounced back with a
shrug of the shoulder and an arching of the mobile
eyebrow.

RALPH: I believe men thought of her in fantasy as
a sister, as well as a mistress or wife. The sister image
was very strong in the 1930's. Anyway we had good
times in the Depression years. People were better be-
haved then. By contrast to the smug and callous wealth
of the 1950's, the sense of a common fate, the humility,
the helpfulness, and humor people used to display during the Depression seem very attractive. The "together-
ness" admired by our contemporary ad-men, therapists,
preachers, and public relations experts is a strictly
phony ethic compared with the feeling of unity which
economic fate generated in us during the thirties.

DOROTHY: I agree with that. But don't forget that
a nostalgia for the 1930's is possible only to those who
never actually suffered or went hungry. It is a common nostalgia nowadays among those of a romantic
and puritanical turn of mind, but I think you will find

it only among middle-class types, often academics, who were not impoverished in the thirties but *are* impoverished, relatively speaking, in the 1950's. Middle-class people of small but secure income, such as professors, actually were better off twenty years ago than they are now. Prices have increased upwards of 100 per cent whereas salaries have increased from 25 to 50 per cent at best. As the keeper of the family budget, I well know that our real income from salaries has steadily decreased since 1940. Obviously, we would benefit greatly, at least for a few years, if a severe and protracted depression should occur to bring prices down. Do you suppose the trustees of universities and schools are content with the fact that those who teach the young are convinced that they have no stake in the continuing prosperity of the country at large? Already these trustees are hiring AB's out of each senior class at beginning salaries equal to what an associate professor is paid after twenty-five years of struggle. The officials at Ralph's university continue to send out engraved cards inviting faculty members to join others of "the University community" at some official dinner or other—$12.50 per plate, black tie. What kind of a world do the university officials live in? Ralph hasn't owned a dinner jacket for fifteen years. And $12.50 a plate would be only the beginning of the evening's expenses, which would also include baby-sitter and transportation.

RALPH: I'm afraid at this rate we will never bring George into the fold. He will take the job with the insurance company the first thing Monday morning.

NANCY: If he doesn't, there will be no more little Middlebys and I will go to work again myself.

RALPH: You have held a job since you were married?

NANCY: I did until my salary began to be exceeded by the costs of baby-sitters, cleaning woman, and nursery school. But if I can get a better job, I can make a go of it. Many of my contemporaries have professional careers despite all the problems involved, without upsetting the children too much or making their husbands feel unduly neglected. The only thing that frightened me was that I began to use my job as a convenient way of not facing the difficulties of raising the children. Herman is very winsome at the age of three, but since I have returned full time to the career of housewife and mother I can see some of the results of having been a part-time mother; he has been a real terror, and his older sister now seems to me to have been much too good all her life; she worries me by being so withdrawn. Still, I suppose there may be many reasons for the way children develop, besides the fact that their mothers are career women.

DOROTHY: If I may say so, professors and other white-collar workers had better pick good women unless they want to wreck their careers on the marital rocks. I think the ideal marriage, fairly common in my day and age, was made by the male petty-bourgeois status-seeker and the idealistic daughter who was rebelling from her well-to-do family and wanted to help the struggling masses. She compromised by helping her struggling husband. The two met, as a friend has put it, while crossing the tracks in opposite directions. Apart from the money question, it is a good idea for the professor's wife to have the ability to follow her own interests so that she won't mind the essentially solitary and sedentary traits of her husband. Needless to say, these interests should not involve the latest fashions and household appliances, unless her own income is larger than that of most professor's wives.

GEORGE: What Dorothy has in effect said is that no one in his right mind should take up professoring and have a family too unless he has an independent income.

When I look at the matter candidly, I conclude that the question of whether or not I should abandon my fledgling academic career for the insurance business is really very simple. It depends on the outcome of my father's will, which is now in probate court. If a small but sufficient income is assured me from that estate, I will go on with the academic career. If it isn't, I will become an insurance man. I will leave it to the country at large to consider whether this is a healthy situation.

NANCY: I'm with George on that. I admire his flexibility.

RALPH: So do I. For although the world has seen more gifted teachers than I, I cannot conceive of doing anything but teach. Besides the satisfactions of working with promising young people, I am desperately attached to the irregular schedule of the academic man. The nine-to-five routine is my idea of something impossible.

GEORGE: Yet a routine is something one can use, for one's equability and steady health. After all, like all forms of life, we are mechanisms, and the automatic functions of life are what attaches us to nature. I have an idea, too, that most professors, all but the laziest and the most creative, dislike the long vacations, and teach during the summer by choice as well as for economic reasons. Don't they all get psychosomatic colds during Christmas vacation?

I don't look with dismay at the prospect of leaving Academe and entering Philistia. I think that there are ever-widening possibilities of making a compromise between the business world and the life of the intelligence. Intellectuals do not nowadays think of teaching as their only choice. One of my ideals is an American culture more nearly like the English or French, in which an intellectual businessman or a lawyer who cultivates or practices the arts is not unheard of. I think we are tending that way. In all but the most hectic and competitive businesses there is a new relaxation, a new humaneness, a newly mature attitude toward the quality and value of Work. The Puritan exaltation of Work has been relaxed. I see on every hand a desire to live well, to enjoy aesthetic pleasures, to cultivate whatever talents one may happen to have. The new business-man of the world is not the hard-driving, die-with-his-boots-on type who never retires. He retires spiritually and emotionally, as it were, by the time he is forty, assuming that by then he is moderately established in his career. He then tries to be the well-rounded man his professors told him he should be when he was in college. I like these new people, so far as I have had a chance to see them, and because they exist I have few qualms about leaving the ivied walls.

RALPH: You make them sound attractive. I must confess, although it may speed you further on your way, that I have never found professors very attractive as a group. They are horribly given to self-pity, whereas actually there is nothing wrong with their plight that a 100 per cent raise wouldn't cure.

GEORGE: I agree with that. Teachers have real griev-ances, but they spend too much time commiserating with each other and totting up the special tribulations of the profession, just like admirals and clergymen.

DOROTHY: You speak of the lessening gap between the academic life and the nonacademic life. Isn't this partly the result of developments within the universi-ties themselves?

GEORGE: Yes. The universities have acquired a new sense of their wider social function. Especially the sci-ence and sociology departments have entered directly into business and public affairs. The academy is show-ing a wider awareness of its responsibility to society as a whole. The professor, as a type, is still with us, but it gets harder and harder to distinguish him from a lawyer, a bureaucrat, or businessman. He dresses well and conventionally; he is no longer "absent-minded." I can see both good and bad in this change of professional attitude, but I imagine Ralph deplores it *in toto*.

RALPH: I am glad to see the professor become a man of the world, at least in the sense that he is newly aware of what the world is like. And certainly it is a good thing that the presumed intelligence and special knowledge of the university should be brought to bear on the problems of society at large. What I do deplore is the effect the new worldliness is having on education. The value of the university depends on its being different from the rest of society, since its function of gaining, organizing, and interpreting knowledge about the world cannot be accomplished without preserving a measure of detachment. Yet the tendency nowadays, abetted by the foundations, is to embark upon a program of social responsibility by stamping out of the university the special characteristics that make it what it is. The unusually gifted or high-spirited student must surely be chagrined to find that the modern American university is not so much a place where he can make exciting discoveries and engage in scholarship, higher education, athletics, and sowing his wild oats, as a drab and joyless training ground or sub-bureaucracy for turning out competent nonentities. In the undergraduate college of my own university, where for two centuries the ideal has been *mens sana in corpore sano* or the well-rounded man, the new ideal is the "Citizen." All over the country, universities and colleges, traditionally supposed to be *by definition* the home of the arts, as well as of the sciences, are building well-endowed Arts Centers. Partly because it is Broadway, Hollywood, and TV money that endows these centers and partly because of the lack of decision and purpose of those who run them, they become merely vocational training schools for conventional middlebrow art and the mass media. Accommodation to the times and the ever-widening sense of the university's responsibility to society are fine—so long as these are not just high-sounding phrases meaning "suicide." For surely in the long run the academy will have nothing to offer the world if it fails to assert, against the many hostile forces that surround it, an intransigent distinctiveness.

NANCY: But it can't be as bad as all that. I mean, *you* remain committed to your university.

RALPH: Oh, by all means. I'm just giving the dark side of the picture. Despite all of one's doubts about the future America that is being prepared for us by centralization and bureaucracy, by suburban and mass culture, and by a burgeoning population, I agree with George that there is still room both in and out of the academy for the life of intelligence. True, the leisure, the quiet, the intellectual stimulus, the social approval, or at least tolerance, that the intellectual needs are not assured in America, even to the extent that they once were—in the days of dear old Longfellow, for example. George and I disagree as to how the intellectual is to make a place for himself in the world, in the schools, and in the family. It strikes me as partly a matter of the ever-fresh stratagem, the ever-new unheroic version of "silence, exile, and cunning." It strikes George as more a matter of meeting the social order on its own footing. We all have to begin with the fact that American culture is not as anti-intellectual as it makes out to be. True, we live in a culture in which 90 per cent of all professors are, for purposes of manners and morals, "anti-intellectual." They will tell you that they are not intellectuals themselves and that those who claim to be are snobs. But the fact remains that all of them, sociologically speaking, and most of them, judged by their mental prowess and habits of mind, obviously *are* intellectuals. Intellectuals, like other minority groups, come in for much resentment and suspicion. And of course there is much hidden demagoguery of a potentially dangerous sort in the recurrent Know-Nothingism of Americans. But we are faced with ambiguity and indecision, not with a monolithic hostility.

GEORGE: Yes, I think professors have an exaggerated notion of the hostility felt toward them. As Lionel Trilling points out, literary people, especially, like to present themselves as isolated and persecuted because this enhances their sense of saintly virginity. Anyway, underneath all the conventional talk about oddballs and reds, there is a genuine respect for professors, as for other intellectuals. Nor is this merely a dwindling remnant of the nineteenth-century opinion which thought of professors as an aristocratic elite automatically entitled to reverence. It is really a new modern attitude, although I will agree with the words that I seem to perceive on the tip of Ralph's tongue: that professors are admired in so far as they can be thought of as technicians, rather than as speculative intellectuals. Also, as Ralph says, modern people in all walks of life have a tremendous need to find "wisdom." Never was wisdom about life, and how to live it, at a higher premium. And to find it people often turn to the professor.

RALPH: Despite the fact that the professor does not, or should not, pretend to wisdom but only to competence in his field, and despite the irrefutable proof that his wisdom about life in general is no more reliable than that of businessmen and prize fighters?

GEORGE: Oh, yes, despite all that. But even if the professor who is in reality a creative intellectual (and many are) is dismayed to find that he is generally thought of as merely a technician of some sort, he should not inquire too closely into what it is that gives him his public status. The important thing is that he has it.

RALPH: True enough. We have learned how to live. We are adept at rebellion, exploitation, and accommodation, as these are required.

Saturday Morning:
The Illusion of the Middle Way

RALPH: Well, George, since you are disposed to converse, let us sit here under the trees while the women and children are in town. The quiet coolness of the goldfish pond is conducive to meditation; it looks almost like a grotto with its canopy of leaves that overhang the rock wall.

GEORGE: We should perhaps perform some kind of rite. In any case, I see a waggish artist has tried with his chisel to imprint upon this lichen-covered rock the features of a whale. And the brown wooden goddess among the trees gives me the sense of being in a sacred grove. She is too thin, though.

RALPH: Well, if you are going to carve a fertility goddess out of a railroad tie, you have to make her thin, providing you are determined to make her six feet tall. Thin as she is, she looks like a real African idol. She is the product of some visiting sculptor who stopped here once in the halcyon days of Fitzpatrick. Various other art works lurk in the shrubbery; we have Florentine urns made of Portland cement; there are lions in the overgrown *allée* on the other side of the house.

GEORGE: Fitzpatrick and his friends seem to have been an odd mixture of corniness and real distinction.

RALPH: Yes, quite in the old fellow-traveling style.

GEORGE: You were offering last night some generalizations about what magazines like the *Partisan Review* call "the cultural situation." You say that you take a dim view of "my generation," assuming for the moment that there is such a thing. Can you enlighten me on these matters?

RALPH: I start with the proposition that in our time there is a general drive, in all segments of our culture, toward some sort of middle ground of taste and opinion, a general desire for passivity and rest and conformity, a fear of the turmoil of the mind, a longing to escape conflict, a longing to assuage all the vivid contradictions and anomalies that in the past have engaged the American mind. The leading image of the day is a sort of mystic centrality, an equability of mind. This middle view of things finds a sanction at its best in the tragic sense of life and in the inherited common sense of the race. At its worst, it finds a sanction in mere complacency, laziness of mind, fear of extreme ideas and feelings. Its most noticeable manifestation is the smothering orthodoxy and conformism of the Eisenhower Age. The search for a middle way of culture is in certain radically significant ways a denial and abandonment of the cultural ideals of the American mind of the past, as this mind is mirrored in our most characteristic historical figures and in our most characteristic and original literature.

GEORGE: A very heady proposition. I don't understand exactly what you are driving at. I start, however, with an impression that your proposition is authentic. Being more optimistic than you, I start also with the belief that despite the undeniable conformism and timidity shown by many aspects of our culture, there is nevertheless emerging a new way of life in which intellectuals will play a more concrete role in the world, in which there will be an abundance of cultural opportunities for that large minority who care about culture at all, and in which complacency will be transmuted into a humane and enlightened receptivity to art and ideas. We shall be free of bohemian extremism; the life of the artist and intellectual will be less abortive and misdirected, less wearing and wasteful; the galling alienations of the past will be absorbed into the intellectual community; we shall get on better and feel ourselves more solidly situated in the daily conditions of our life. The intellectuals will more and more accept America and America will accept the intellectuals.

I don't want to sound blissful and utopian. I just give you my sense of the way things are actually tending. As for the past, what do you mean precisely by "the American mind" or "the American imagination"? Frankly, I have always felt like the eminent literary critic whom I once heard saying of a speech he was about to deliver at the Indiana School of Letters: "Thank God, I don't have to deal with 'the American mind.'" In this, as in everything, the critic, an extremist and highbrow in his view of poetry and politics, struck me as being very American indeed.

RALPH: I don't pretend to know what "the American mind" is, but I do think that American culture has always operated according to a dialectic that can be defined.

GEORGE: I have never thought that was true. In fact I have often doubted if properly speaking there has been an American culture. I realize, of course, that there are certain characteristic American attitudes, ways of speech, a certain folklore of thought and behavior. There are chewing gum, skyscrapers, baseball, Mark Twain. But I would think our literary and intellectual culture has always been mostly European. We are like the Romans, whose culture was Greek. Then too, it seems to me that in order to have a "culture" you must have a "nation." And I agree with Edmund Wilson, who says in *A Piece of My Mind* that "America is not a nation, in the sense that England and France are nations. It is a society, a political system."

RALPH: Yes, I think Wilson is right about that. Still, I think that under the pressure of environment and inherited habit European culture has been in many ways Americanized in this country and that by now our shared experiences, feelings, and intellectual responses have long since consolidated into a complex of attitudes for which there is no adequate word but culture. If you will allow me the necessary word, I will try to suggest to you some of its leading qualities. And if, finally, you grant me that this complex of attitudes is sufficiently definable as something that exists, you must grant me the word "culture" without reservations.

GEORGE: Agreed. Lead on.

RALPH: I have stated my proposition about the present situation and what seems to me its potentially disastrous departure from inherited experience. At least it seems to me that a "disaster" occurs if a country finally abandons its radical, creative past and settles down into a sterile complacency. But by way of leading back to my first proposition, allow me to present a second: Among the most perceptive observers of American life the most influential are those who (1) tell us that our culture has always been marked by striking differences, even outright contradictions, of taste and opinion, as between what may be provisionally called high culture and low culture, and (2) view this split with alarm and advocate a middle ground in which contradictions and differences may be reconciled.

GEORGE: I begin to see what you are getting at, and just to keep my own head clear, let me say that I agree both with the diagnosis and the cure proposed by your "perceptive observers."

RALPH: I agree only with the diagnosis. For as it

seems to me, it is the duty of the intellectual these days to oppose, or at least to question, the ideal of a middle culture, as our best writers and thinkers have always done—whether they were lone voices crying in the wilderness or, being more fortunate, could find some companionship in a concerted avant-garde movement. At present there is no real opposition, and this is the era of the triumphant middle. The fact remains, however, that a middle way can be established only by losing contact with certain of the basic realities of our civilization. This has not been understood by the above-mentioned observers.

GEORGE: I imagine the first critic you have in mind is Tocqueville.

RALPH: Yes, in his *Democracy in America* Tocqueville tried to account for a number of related contradictions in American life. He noted a disparity between ideals and practice, a lack of connection between thought and experience, a tendency of the American mind to oscillate rather wildly between ideas that "are all either extremely minute and clear or extremely general and vague."

Tocqueville sought a genetic explanation for these disparities. He pointed out that in aristocratic societies there was a shared body of inherited habits, attitudes, and institutions that stood in a mediating position between the individual and the state. This, he observed, was not true in a democracy, where "each citizen is habitually engaged in the contemplation of a very puny object; namely, himself." If he ever looks higher, Tocqueville says, he perceives only "the immense form of society at large or the still more imposing aspect of mankind. . . . What lies between is a void." Tocqueville believed that this either/or habit of mind also owed much to the sharp distinctions made by Calvinism and its habit of opposing the individual to his God, with a minimum of mythic or ecclesiastical mediation.

GEORGE: Of course Calvinism has been a tremendous influence. But some people talk as if it were still a force in America. Is it?

RALPH: I think so. It left on American thought a deep impression that survived the liberalization and secularization of the churches. In a way it was hardly Christian to begin with—it was Manichaean. Yvor Winters and others have pointed out that Calvinism strongly affected the imagination of writers like Hawthorne and Melville and entered deeply into the national consciousness, re-emerging, for example, in the ideology of Populism. From the historical point of view, the primitive New England Puritanism was a momentous backsliding in religion. For at least as apprehended by the popular and the literary imagination, this Puritanism—with its grand metaphors of election and damnation, its opposition of the Kingdom of Light and the Kingdom of Darkness, its eternal and autonomous contraries of good and evil—seems to have recaptured the Manichaean sense of things. As it expresses itself in literature, the American imagination, like the New England Puritan mind itself, seems less interested in redemption than in the melodrama of the eternal struggle between good and evil, less interested in incarnation and reconciliation than in alienation and disorder. To this "Manichaean" imagination one may trace the prevalence in American literature of the symbolism of light and dark, a symbolism that has been burned into the mind of every American by the racial composition of our people and the Civil War that was fought over the Negro.

Tocqueville found certain advantages in the "democratic" habit of mind, but he warned Americans that it might well produce great confusion in philosophy, morals, and politics, and a basic instability in literary and cultural values, and that consequently Americans should try to discover democratic equivalents for those traditional habits of mind which in aristocracies had moderated and reconciled extremes in thought and experience.

GEORGE: Yet in saying "democratic" habit of mind, Tocqueville meant to refer in a general way to the whole of Western civilization in modern times, not just to America.

RALPH: Oh, yes. Tocqueville knew that the either/ or kind of thought of which he spoke was specifically American only in the peculiar quality of its origin and expression. He saw that with the probable exception of England, Europe would characteristically concern itself during the nineteenth century with grand intellectual oppositions, often of a Hegelian order. But even though the tendency of thought Tocqueville predicated belonged to Western culture generally, one is nevertheless struck by how often American writers conceive of human dilemmas according to his scheme, and how many make aesthetic and moral capital out of what seemed to him an intellectual shortcoming.

GEORGE: Besides Hawthorne and Melville, what writers have you in mind? Perhaps Henry Adams?

RALPH: Certainly Adams, and many others, including some who seem little concerned with Calvinism or sin, such as Emerson and Whitman.

GEORGE: Emerson is a man of significant oppositions?

RALPH: Yes. In referring to Emerson as having "a Greek head on right Yankee shoulders," in calling him a "Plotinus-Montaigne," James Russell Lowell put his finger on the essential duality of Emerson's thought and character. Emerson was himself acutely conscious of this duality throughout his life. He contemplated it with alternating (or, as he would say, compensatory)

changes of attitude, sometimes seeing in it a challenge
to spirited dialectics, sometimes beholding it with baffled and stoic acquiescence. Not surprisingly, the more
sanguine attitude characterizes the great essays of the
1830's and '40's and the acquiescent attitude characterizes the writings of the later years. In his book on
Emerson, Stephen Whicher points out that the train of
thought which led Emerson as a young man to the general view that, as he expressed it, "man is conscious of
a twofold nature which manifests itself in perpetual
self-contradiction" was, despite Emerson's learning,
"substantially a fresh insight of his own." The idea of
duality seems to have been as native to Emerson as it
was to Whitman, who wrote in an early notebook, "I
cannot understand the mystery, but I am always conscious of myself as two." Whicher suggests that Emerson's early struggles with the dilemmas of the thinker
in an emerging democracy seem so native to his time
and place that they have something of the quality of
"primitive painting."

It has become clear to the modern Emerson scholars,
by the way, that he by no means entirely escaped the
Calvinism of his ancestors. In giving up the mild ethi-
cism of the Unitarians he not only progressed to a
vigorous poetics and ethics of the self; by inverting,
rather than merely rejecting, such tenets of Calvinism
as the belief in eternal damnation, he retained much
of the Puritan spirit, and in several ways the Puritan
mode of thought. Whicher says that Emerson did not
heal the Calvinist division between God and man by
assuming that God was in the human self; he merely
made an objective dualism subjective. He endowed
man with "double consciousness," indeed with "two
selfs." In the period of his great early essays, the "Satur-
nalia" of his freshly achieved transcendentalist faith,
Emerson could exclaim with scarcely less bravado than

Whitman, "Do I contradict myself?/ Very well then I contradict myself." Incidentally, let's remember that when Whitman uttered these famous—to many people notorious—words in "Song of Myself," he was not referring so much to mere verbal or logical contradictions as to contradictions contained within the self—or, to put it another way, he was referring to contradictory selves.

GEORGE: All this is new to me, and I confess you and Mr. Whicher are performing the unlikely feat of arousing in me an interest in Emerson. I like some of Emerson's apothegms, yet he composed so much by the sentence that what he wants to say never seems to me to get marshaled into any sort of sensible paragraphs or essays. He does have, as you suggest, exuberance and vitality. Yet he seems unfortunately cold, aloof, quirky, eccentric. A man given so much to solipsism needs a heavy ballast of factuality to keep him on the ground. And he needs a fixed lens to keep the self in focus against the background of the not-self. I remember reading his mad essay on "The Tragic." There never was a mind less aware of tragedy, or of a morally structured universe.

RALPH: I would not, for the moment, wish to hold either his eccentricity or his lack of the tragic sense against him. And I fear that whatever the universe is, it is not morally structured—I understood you last night to say it is not.

Yet there is substance to your doubts about Emerson. I imagine that what we both miss in Emerson is context, continuity, system, but above all context (for much may be done without the other two). What do contradictions matter or tell us if they exist in a realm somewhere over our heads and are not brought down into relation with the human, social, and historical facts they purport to refer to—as, in their differing ways,

Hawthorne, Melville, and Whitman bring their perception of contradictions into significant context. It is not that Emerson neglects to observe facts—"the meal in the firkin; the milk in the pan; the ballad in the street; the news of the boat; the glance of the eye; the form and gait of the body."

GEORGE: Oh, he observes facts, but my trouble is that we are invited to see these facts in relation to some sort of sublime presence or high spiritual cause, to which Emerson immediately leaps, without telling us why the meal is in the firkin or what we have to gain by thinking of it as a hieroglyphic of that so extremely distant spiritual cause.

RALPH: "The American Scholar" is comparatively concrete. There he notices the celebrated and problematic split between theory and practice, intelligence and action. He notes that "the so-called 'practical men' sneer at speculative men," and he believes that this is a culturally dangerous alienation. But despite the pragmatic social intention of Emerson's transcendentalism, the dialectic of cultural opposites suggested in "The American Scholar" had to wait for its full exposition until Van Wyck Brooks' *America's Coming-of-Age*. In this essay, Brooks did much to define the implications of Emerson's rather vague cultural criticism, beginning as he did, with the assumption that Emerson is so often "abstract at the wrong times and concrete at the wrong times" and that he "was imperfectly interested in human life."

GEORGE: Brooks' words stick in the mind. I read *America's Coming-of-Age* in the army, improbable as that may seem. But does Emerson advocate "a middle way"?

RALPH: In his later thinking especially he concerns himself with the problem of reconciling contradictions, of finding "the temperate zone" which is in "the middle region of our being." Thus the elaborate and often fantastic array of "compensations," "undulations," "hieroglyphics," "circles," and "scales," which we come across in his essays. But when Emerson was great he was vividly conscious of polarities and oppositions, of what he called "the extremities and suburbs" of experience. As Whicher says, the power of his writing stems from the "compulsions and conflicts, the revelations and the doubts, the glories and the fears" which stirred his imagination and urged him to definition. These compulsions and conflicts, and not the search for a "temperate zone," are the origin of Emerson's great poetry of the self.

GEORGE: I certainly grant to Emerson a "great poetry of the self." But Brooks is one of the "perceptive critics" you spoke of?

RALPH: Very much so. But first, there is Henry Adams—and some others. As Adams tells us in the *Education*, he had from the beginning a "double consciousness." Do you recall his account of the origins of this habit of mind in the first chapter of the *Education?* It is one of the classics of American literature.

GEORGE: You mean where he speaks of "the harshness of contrasts" and "the extremes of sensibility" that characterize the New England weather and the New England moral life?

RALPH: Exactly. He goes on to say that "Winter and summer, cold and heat, town and country, force and freedom, marked two modes of life and thought, balanced like lobes of the brain. . . . The bearing of the two seasons on the education of Henry Adams was no fancy; it was the most decisive force he ever knew; it ran through life, and made the division between its perplexing, warring, irreconcilable problems, irreducible opposites, with growing emphasis to the last year of study. From earliest childhood, the boy was accustomed to feel that, for him, life was double."

Thus did his surroundings give to Adams the habit of mind which he would later understand as coming to him from his Calvinist as well as his democratic heritage. It was as much forced upon him by the past as by the time in which he was born—a time, as he saw it, in which the Adams tradition of political leadership was rendered obsolete by the widening split in American affairs between intelligence and action.

GEORGE: And you think of Adams' "education" as an attempt to find out how to heal such gaps?

RALPH: In part, yes. Like many Americans of his time—like the Whitman of *Democratic Vistas*, like Edward Bellamy in *Looking Backward*—Adams made the assumption that the danger to American democracy was inner disharmony and chaos, and he set himself to remedy what he conceived to be an explosively dangerous situation by seeking for modes of harmony and unity. To me this seems to have been a misconception, and I agree with that side of Tocqueville's analysis which holds that in the long run the danger to American democracy is not too much disunion but too much union, too much harmony, too much crushing and burdensome conformity. The ever-present danger, more apparent now than in the aftermath of the Civil War, is not explosive anarchy but stagnation and stasis, not too little synthesis, but too much. One thus follows Adams' search for the Virgin—the symbol of cultural harmony—with the utmost interest and fascination, but with an ever-increasing sense of its irrelevance to American culture. Reading the final chapters of the *Education*, one hears in the despairing tone of Adams' apocalyptic poetry of forces—hardly less vague than Emerson's transcendentalism—the cry of one more American who has allowed himself to be reduced to a futile irony by his galling sense of polarity. Adams is the most famous example of the modern American Hamlet, whose character and thought are finally neutralized by contradictions, rather than being inspirited and enlivened by them. His education ends in symbol and myth, rather than in dialectic and historical realism—although I do not deny the great value of what has been called Adams' "cleansing pessimism."

GEORGE: I am much impressed and somewhat overpowered by the unexpected range and intent of your generalizations. I begin to see many new possibilities of talking about American life and letters. At the same time, I have doubts whether such an ambitious dialectic can remain close enough to the observable facts to express and rationalize them. But for the moment I am content merely to register this doubt. You spoke of American Hamlets. It occurs to me that Russian literature boasts many such characters, notably the stories of Turgenev and Chekhov. But I suppose Stavrogin in Dostoievski's *Possessed* is the most extreme example of the man reduced to impotence, despair, and finally suicide by the contradictions of his temperament and of his views. Have we any American Stavrogins?

RALPH: I think we have had many, although their agony has been more private, more personal and concealed, less universally significant than that of Stavrogin or of his prototype, Hamlet. Our Americans are more like Nejdanov in Turgenev's *Virgin Soil.* I would mention two who have interested me. In literature, Melville; in real life, F. O. Matthiessen. These two very different men were alike in this—in their inner being they were finally exhausted and neutralized by the contradictions they contained. Contradiction, which in the healthy organism results in wit, vital versatility, and a strategy for dealing successfully with the confusing assault of reality upon the ego, produced in them a

deep fatigue that left them mere shells of men. The
first thing one noticed about Matthiessen in his last
years, fine scholar and friend that he was, was the un-
canny lack of self, of inner resiliency, of interior hum
and buzz. In less extreme form many Americans are
like that. Few have the final power, or desperation, to
emulate Matthiessen's symbolic leap from the hotel
window.

GEORGE: I remember reading the sad report one
Sunday morning in the *Times*. What was the symbolic
intent?

RALPH: Apparently to assert a spiritual solidarity
with Jan Masaryk, the son of the hero of Czechoslovak
democracy, who died in a similar way. It was perhaps
also a gesture against McCarthyism.

But to turn for a moment to the American novelists
and poets, it is obvious that when they are at their
characteristic best, they conceive of experience in its
contradictoriness. Hawthorne and Melville, one might
almost say, derived their understanding of human nature and formed the very quality of their art and imagination from their persistent sense of an opposition
between the head and the heart. To allow the cold,
dispassionate intellect to get out of touch with human
impulse and the genial emotions was for Hawthorne so
great a moral error that he called it the "unpardonable
sin." At the same time the dialectical alienation of the
elements of human nature and experience is the in-
forming principle of his art of romance. The same may
be said of Melville, whose Captain Ahab pronounces
the summary word on himself by saying that he is
"damned most malignantly" because he has "the high
perception" but lacks "the low enjoying power."

And then there is Whitman, who for so long was ac-
cused of totally lacking the sort of tension and inner
drama that are generated by conflict. It is now clear,

however, that his vision of things, when it is not merely "mystic," really consists of a sustained tension of contraries—Whitman who says that the soul has "measureless sympathy" and "measureless pride" but that in poetry, whose "inmost secrets sleep with the twain," "the one balances the other."

And do we not see something characteristic in T. S. Eliot's idea that since the seventeenth century the Western mind has been increasingly split between intellect and emotion, so that a "dissociation of sensibility" has occurred? One may predict that when the present state of the critical mind changes and shifts away from its exaggerated preoccupation with symbol, myth, tragedy, incarnation—with modes, that is, of reconciliation and centrality—a true and illuminating study of Eliot will be written to show his kinship with the Calvinist-Manichee strain of thought in America. He will then be seen to be a skeptic to the last and to have an imagination that responds most characteristically to forms of alienation and disorder. Eliot is, by instinct, more the romancer and melodramatist than the tragic Christian poet. He is a Christian poet *manqué*.

GEORGE: I am in danger of being stupefied by these rapid abstractions. I follow you perfectly through Hawthorne and Melville. What you say about Eliot I accept as a mental *jeu d'esprit*. But I want to hear more about Whitman. What you say about him seems, frankly, all wrong. Do you really find any inner drama and tension in that sublime windbag?

RALPH: Yes, certainly. But will you let me come round to Whitman by way of D. H. Lawrence and Van Wyck Brooks, both of whom have misrepresented Whitman in the process of saying many illuminating things about American culture? But first a historical observation. The tendency to think of American culture in terms of an inner dialectic of contraries, and then to advocate on moral grounds the search for a middle way, was carried over into the first decades of this century. The critics of this period succeeded in giving their critique a much larger measure of concrete relevance than had been done previously. In *Studies in Classic American Literature*, D. H. Lawrence presented his version of the contrariety or, as he said, "duplicity" of the American literary mind by saying that he found in our writers "a tight mental allegiance to a morality which all their passion goes to destroy." He was thinking of an inherent conflict between "genteel" Puritan spirituality and a pragmatic experientialism which in its lower depths was sheer Dionysian, or "Indian," energy and violence. Acute enough to see that the best American artistic achievements had depended in one way or another on this dualism, he seemed ready nevertheless to advocate, on moral grounds, a reconciliation of opposites. Lawrence says that Whitman was the first great American writer to point the way toward the necessary reconciliation of spirit and matter, intelligence and instinct. As he expressed it, "Whitman was the first to break the mental allegiance. He was the first to smash the old moral conception, that the soul of man is something 'superior' and 'above' the flesh. Even Emerson still maintained that tiresome 'superiority' of the soul. Even Melville could not get over it. Whitman was the first heroic seer to seize the soul by the scruff of her neck and plant her down among the potsherds." So far so good. But Whitman does not say to the soul, as Lawrence makes him say, "There, stay there!" What Whitman really says is: "*Don't* stay there! Fly free, disentangle, define yourself as soul and not as potsherd, and when you get too uppity or too thin and hungry for want of life among the potsherds, I'll plant you down again." When his mind is working properly, Whitman is a free spirit, a dialectician. And now for Brooks. You say you admire *America's Coming-of-Age?*

GEORGE: Yes. I think it is a brilliant philippic; it is *verbally* brilliant, full of witty sayings and memorable phrases. Still, the book strikes me as being almost absurdly ambitious in its cultural formulations. Brooks' argument is too extreme, too vauntingly tendentious for me—or so it seemed, reading it in the noncontemplative atmosphere of Camp Edwards.

RALPH: Let us see if you will agree with my summary of *America's Coming-of-Age.* It was in this essay, published in 1915, that Brooks made his celebrated and useful division of American culture into "highbrow" and "lowbrow." Brooks' ultimate aim was to discover and define a cultural middle ground whereon he hoped to establish a moderating "organic" intelligence and imagination. His main thesis is the split between intelligence and experience, spirituality and realism, that runs through our history, beginning with two contemporaries, Jonathan Edwards (the highbrow) and Franklin (the lowbrow). Brooks was worried by this split. He made some acute comments on the desiccation and overrefinement of the highbrow who had intelligence but was unable to bring it to bear on experience. He pointed out the tendency of the lowbrow to be resourceful, pragmatic, and inventive, but also his tendency to be subservient to the shibboleths of chauvinism, mass thinking, and material success and his irreconcilable hostility to intellect. (In calling Franklin a lowbrow, as you see, Brooks had in mind the Poor Richard side of Franklin, rather than the *philosophe.*) At the time Brooks wrote, Woodrow Wilson and William Jennings Bryan were handy symbols of the highbrow-lowbrow opposition, as later were to be Dr. J. Robert Oppenheimer and Senator McCarthy. To remedy the situation, Brooks proposed a new intelligentsia, a new group of dedicated spirits who, mediating between separated segments of our culture, would establish a middle way which would deal with our forms of cultural confusion, alienation, and discontinuity by absorbing them into an "organic" whole.

This is where Whitman comes in. Do you remember what Brooks says? He says, "we have the rudiments of a middle tradition, a tradition that effectively combines theory and action, a tradition just as fundamentally American as either flag-waving or money-grabbing, one that is visibly growing but which has already been grossly abused; and this is the tradition that begins with Walt Whitman. The real significance of Whitman is that he, for the first time, gave us the sense of something organic in American life." Brooks goes on to describe Whitman as "a great vegetable of a man, all of a piece in roots, flavor, substantiality and succulence, well ripened in the common sunshine. In him the hitherto incompatible extremes of the American temperament were fused. The refinement of the Puritan tradition, summed up as an original type in Jonathan Edwards, able to make nothing of a life so rude in its actuality, turned for its outlet to a disembodied world, the shadow world of Emerson, Hawthorne, and Poe, a world fastidiously intellectual in which only two colors exist, white and black. Whitman was the Antaeus of this tradition who touched earth with it and gave it hands and feet. For having all the ideas of New England, being himself saturated with Emersonianism, he came up from the other side with everything New England did not possess: quantities of rude feeling and a faculty of gathering humane experience almost as great as that of the hero of the *Odyssey*." "Whitman," says Brooks, "precipitated the American character." He became for us the "focal center"

which "is the first requisite of a great people." Yet,
Brooks adds, Whitman tended to be beyond his depth
"on the plane of ideas" and his "social ideal" remains
"essentially a collection of raw materials molten and
malleable, which take shape only in an emotional
form." Consequently it is the duty of the new intelligentsia, for which Brooks calls, to articulate and explain
Whitman's "middle tradition." This is Brooks' main
mistake.

Whitman is not an enormous middlebrow cabbage.
He does not dissolve and reconcile in his succulent
emotional juices the contradictions of his culture.
When he makes sense as a poet or a social critic he
does so exactly by his ability to objectify and illustrate
those very contradictions. It is no longer possible to
suppose that Whitman is the "focal center" of our civilization. What Brooks had in mind is shown by his link-
ing, in this respect, Virgil, Mazzini, and Björnson with
Whitman. He had in mind, that is, small relatively ho-
mogeneous countries and the cultural situation that
arises in such countries during intensely nationalistic
eras, such as the nineteenth century. But America is
"trans-national," as Brooks' valuable friend Randolph
Bourne wrote. America is cosmopolitan, immense.
There is no "focal center" of our cultural life. No writer,
no matter how great or vague in outline, can be the
sort of symbolic image of centrality Brooks saw in
Whitman. Our writers embody our culture to the extent that they embody its contradictions. There are
many ways of doing this, besides the Whitman way.

But Brooks' diagnosis remains of permanent value.
His early writings isolated and defined for the first time
the nature of a realistic criticism of American culture.
He showed us the way. His error was to conclude that
all departments of our civilization would benefit by a
reconciliation of extremes. Actually, there were good

reasons for coming to this conclusion in 1915. At that time it was impossible not to see a rather frightening void between the highbrow and the lowbrow. But now the void, like a hungry vacuum, has long since been filled to the point of surfeit and suffocation. Forgive me for making a lecture. The whole question strikes me as very important.

GEORGE: No, no—I don't object to your lecturing. I, too, think the subject is important. I agree in a general way with what you have said. Still, I feel that like Brooks you weaken your argument to some extent by your tendency to play a kind of abstract game in which the counters are words like highbrow and lowbrow, the steps in the playing of the game being negotiated by analogy and metaphor. In other words, your argument seems to me to be cogent only at a high level of abstraction. I feel that we should abandon terms like highbrow and lowbrow.

RALPH: I'm glad to hear you say that, not because I agree with you but because it gives me a chance to find out what people mean when they make this proposal. Do you mean that we ought to give up those terms because they do not refer to cultural realities? Or do you mean that they *do* refer to cultural realities but that the cultivated man should be neither exclusively highbrow nor lowbrow—or perhaps that the cultivated man should be a little of both?

GEORGE: I have not thought it out as carefully as I should have. But I mean to include everything implied by your questions. That is, I believe that in the 1950's a basic change is beginning to overtake American cultural life which will gradually render terms like highbrow and lowbrow irrelevant, however accurately they may still be used in referring to the past. Also I believe that the ideally cultivated man should be freely versatile in his tastes and opinions.

RALPH: Long live versatility! To be versatile, to be a Jack-of-all-trades like Melville's Ishmael, has been, until recent times, one of the distinctive American traits—but only in practical life and the useful crafts. In matters of art, as in moral attitudes, Americans have been deplorably inflexible in their tastes and commitments. How ridiculous that Henry James and Mark Twain, two of our literary grandees who shared more than they knew, should have had so little understanding of each other.

As for the basic change you say is coming into American life, I don't know whether to believe you or not. I don't hesitate to say that I instinctively resist and dislike it. If it is really coming about, I should prefer to share your obvious receptivity toward it.

Meanwhile, I propose that since we are willy-nilly stuck with "highbrow" and associated terms, we try to define them.

GEORGE: A highbrow is a longhair. He likes Bach and Stravinsky but not *My Fair Lady*. He likes Joyce but not James Gould Cozzens. He is fastidious and snobbish and puts on the airs of a superior intelligence, which he may or may not possess. He is "advanced" in the realm of art and ideas but is ignorant of real life —I'm not satisfied with this definition, by the way, but am content for the moment to give you the ordinarily accepted picture. A lowbrow is a televiewer who watches Ed Sullivan because he finds Steve Allen too intellectual. He likes Elvis Presley or, if he is older, Lawrence Welk and Liberace. He likes automobiles that look like juke boxes, refrigerators, or jet planes. When he says "book" he means either comic book or a volume with "How To . . ." on the cover. He may read the *Saturday Evening Post*, but *The New Yorker* is too deep for him.

RALPH: Very good. But let's define these terms apart

from mannerisms and particular tastes and choices. Think of them, for the moment, as intellectual rather than as sociological categories. In this sense, a highbrow is a man with an ideal of disinterested intelligence who makes strong demands on our powers of attention, reason, sensibility, and seriousness. A lowbrow is a man whose sense of things has been formed by the give and take of life, and whose ideas come from inherited folk wisdom, folk art, or folk prejudice, or from the myths conveyed to him by the mass media or by the lodge, legion, or union to which he belongs.

GEORGE: And a middlebrow?

RALPH: He is by nature indefinable except in terms of other things that *can* be defined. He puts on a protective coloration under which we see the attempt to resist definition by foregoing all the hazards of a highbrow or lowbrow view. The protective coloration suggests a general benignity, powerlessness, and belief in moderation, an attitude of being bewildered by life, a belief in the virtue of gentle, wistful humor. Yet despite his characteristic attitude of mildness and lack of aggressive impulse, the middlebrow paradoxically claims nothing less than to be the custodian of the vital mainstream of enlightenment, common sense, and humane civilization—a stream which he proposes to protect from highbrow and lowbrow pollution.

GEORGE: There are good ways and bad ways of being a highbrow or a lowbrow?

RALPH: Certainly. The characteristic flaw of the former is sterility, and of the latter, Know Nothingism.

GEORGE: I suspect you've got it in for the middlebrows. You speak as if there were something furtive or ashamed about middlebrowism. Is there?

RALPH: Yes, it comes from the fundamental insecurity of being an intellectual anti-intellectual—for that, in a nutshell, is what the middlebrow is. Yet even so noncommittal a view of things is capable, by a very great intellectual effort, of profound articulation and refinement.

GEORGE: You mean it is possible in this country to be an admirable middlebrow?

RALPH: Yes, but it is much easier to be an admirable highbrow or lowbrow.

GEORGE: These are sociohistorical terms, aren't they? I mean they don't have a transcendent validity.

RALPH: Correct. Only by way of analogy can one use the terms highbrow, middlebrow, and lowbrow to refer to cultural attitudes and works of art of more than a few decades ago. To be sure, the kinds of taste and attitude one associates with, for example, middlebrow writers of our own time are to be seen in literary works of various times and places throughout history. Thus it makes some sense to say that Chaucer was a middlebrow, whereas the French romancers and allegorists who gave him many of his ideas were highbrow, just as one might say that Pascal was a highbrow and Montaigne a middlebrow. But because these terms are not only aesthetic and intellectual but also sociohistorical categories, they refer with full accuracy only to the modern times that have given rise to them. They are inevitably associated with the absorption of art and literature by commercialism and bureaucracy and the consequent emergence of a middle ground of culture, which in America in the time of Howells began to occupy the gap between the high culture and the low culture that had existed since the eighteenth century.

The "brow" terms first began to be consistently used about forty years ago by Brooks and other critics who wanted to counter this absorption of culture with the concerted effort of a militant intelligentsia or avant-garde whose purpose it was to defend radical values. For a time the highbrow—for example, Waldo Frank

—made common cause with the lowbrow—like Sherwood Anderson—against the gathering flood of middlebrowism. But at present this sort of collaboration of the extremes has largely broken down.

GEORGE: The whole question of the avant-garde interests me. The avant-garde is dead, wouldn't you say?

RALPH: Under modern conditions the avant-garde is a permanent movement. It is only in its recent long phase that it is dead. But let us postpone this matter to another time, along with the whole question of whether there is the possibility or desirability of a radical attitude toward life these days, and to what extent a cultural radicalism needs to be or can be political radicalism. For the moment, let me merely observe that in the realm of politics, as Tocqueville predicted, America has always tended to allow a potentially dangerous split between intelligence and action, and that a firm middle way must be perpetually re-established. But Brooks' case for a middle way in the realm of art, manners, and morals, which we call culture, now seems untenable.

Nothing could be clearer than that in the last forty years, as throughout our history, our writers have been great as highbrows (Eliot, Wallace Stevens), lowbrows (Dreiser, Sherwood Anderson, Frost), or as combination highbrow-lowbrows (Faulkner and Hemingway—like Melville and Whitman before them).

You will notice that middlebrow critics and scholars are particularly baffled by this last category. The trouble is that they do not conceive how a writer like Faulkner can keep up such a lively dialectic oscillation between very sophisticated and very vulgar and earthy kinds of experience, how he emulates both Joyce and local American humor, how, in short, he is always passing through the middlebrow's limited purview without

ever resigning from the hazards of the journey in order
to settle down there. (The extreme opposites in Faulkner's mind are made to engage in a moving, fraternal
colloquy in *Light in August,* in the person of the two
friends, the Reverend Hightower, the intellectual, and
Byron Bunch, the ordinary man, whom Faulkner seems
to have modeled to some extent on those perennial
archetypes, Don Quixote and Sancho Panza.

GEORGE: I'm not sure that even after our effort to
define them, the terms we are using are capable of
making very accurate discriminations. You call Sherwood Anderson a lowbrow, but he was a reader of
Joyce and a rather self-conscious bohemian.

RALPH: In calling Anderson a lowbrow and Faulkner a lowbrow-highbrow, I mean to point to the fact
that Faulkner, like Hemingway, Melville, or Whitman,
meets high culture on its own ground, as in his reading
of Joyce. But in a book like *Dark Laughter,* where Anderson tries to imitate Joyce in some passages, we see
that he has no real sense of Joyce's genius and that his
sense of high culture and the bohemian life is stub-
bornly the lowbrow's sense. Of course it is no longer
possible to take literally Faulkner's pose of simon-pure
lowbrowism, a standard pose of American writers beginning with Whitman.

GEORGE: That is certainly true. But I'm still troubled
by your use of terms, and I think I see now what troubles me—an indecision, which you share with Brooks,
as to whether your terms are merely literary and intellectual or are also sociological. You said a minute ago
that highbrow and lowbrow are aesthetic and intellectual categories and that they are "sociohistorical"
categories too. Now, this means, I take it, that we must
judge writers and artists according to the quality of
their thought and expression and that in doing so
we must take into consideration the social conditions

that in some measure determined the quality of their thought and expression.

RALPH: Yes.

GEORGE: But do you also mean that highbrow and lowbrow refer not only to intellectuals and to literary and artistic people but also to other groups in our society? I will amend the question by limiting it to lowbrows, assuming that a highbrow is by definition an intellectual.

RALPH: Shall we also exclude the middlebrow, on the ground that he too is more or less of an intellectual? There is no middlebrow body or class of people in our population except those who have a certain degree of education and intellectual power and who live by their intelligence. Naturally, they are mostly to be found among the professional classes—the teachers, journalists, publishers, lawyers, doctors, and so on.

GEORGE: Agreed. It is apparently the lowbrows who present the problem. Who are they?

RALPH: I have been using "lowbrow" in the intellectual and literary sense rather than strictly the sociological. One reason for this is a desire to be as clear as possible, to keep the subject within manageable bounds, and to avoid venturing on broader sociological problems which, though they might be interesting and relevant, would lead us too far afield.

GEORGE: Yes, but in citing Brooks it seems to me you began in a largely sociological context and that in going on with your own analysis you have shifted into a literary context without acknowledging the shift. For example, how do you get from Franklin to Sherwood Anderson? What is gained by calling two such different people lowbrows?

Like many people, I associate with the word "lowbrow" that which is nonartistic and nonliterary, or perhaps I should say subartistic and subliterary. As I've said, it makes me think of Elvis Presley fans, the readers of comic books, the mass TV audience, and the numberless people from Maine to California who idolize their fantastically finned cars and simonize them with loving reverence every Sunday morning, or pay someone else to. In its broadest sense I think of "lowbrow" as referring to the unenlightened population of America in general, who live out their lives without ever committing themselves to or even understanding the origins, the hereditary traditions, and the ideal goals of their country or of mankind. They are the barbarians, the rootless hordes in our midst—the vast *lumpen* population. Of course they are not only the poorer people. They are to be found in all economic classes; actually their attitudes seem to be typically those of the new rich.

Now, if these people are indeed lowbrows, how come they don't read the authors you call lowbrow, like Anderson, Dreiser, and Frost? I don't believe they are any more likely to read *Winesburg, Ohio* or *Jennie Gerhardt* or *West-Running Brook* than they are to read *Hamlet* or *Finnegans Wake*. Perhaps that isn't a fair question—but what is it these writers have in common with the barbarians?

RALPH: Their instinctive hostility to intellect, art, and culture. Their substitution of the clichés and myths of popular superstition for knowledge.

GEORGE: And do Poor Richard, William Jennings Bryan, Senator McCarthy, Sherwood Anderson, Dreiser, Frost, Elvis Presley, and the idolators of finned automobiles all meet these requirements?

RALPH: With proper qualifications, yes.

GEORGE: But Anderson's *Winesburg*, for example, is a work of great subtlety. It has many exquisite touches and insights. It breathes a spirit of love for mankind and offers a liberating and rewarding experience to the reader. Doesn't this make Anderson a middlebrow or highbrow?

RALPH: No, it makes him a fine novelist. A lowbrow attitude toward culture doesn't disqualify one as an artist; on the contrary, there is a lowbrow, more or less concealed, in most great artists. The gift of talent or genius is what differentiates the people you just mentioned, but this gift is inscrutable; we cannot understand its powers of transmutation.

Now tell me, are the local cop, priest, and grocer lowbrows? Are Postmaster General Summerfield and all the other typical businessmen across the country lowbrows?

GEORGE: I begin to see that the term becomes too vague if we apply it to everyone who is uneducated or unreflective. Apparently one qualifies as a highbrow, middlebrow, or lowbrow not primarily by the degree of one's education or intelligence, but rather by the life-style or cultural persona one asserts.

RALPH: Correct. It is a matter of cultural animus and ideology. Since we have in this country no fixed hereditary class distinctions, every man is free to assume his own life-style. The urge to define oneself as having a certain attitude toward intelligence and as having certain tastes and preferences has become stronger and stronger as America derives more and more of its values from the economy of consumption that has followed the older economy of production. Only when people publicly assert a given range of taste and opinion do the "brow" terms become relevant. And this cultural assertion, whether it is a matter of mere animus or of ideology, whether we detect it in a person's manners and morals or in his articulate self-apology, goes on restlessly beneath the placid surface of conformity. On the whole this urge to cultural differentiation is a good thing, although it sometimes generates mistrust and misunderstanding. I personally think the middlebrow animosities have been the most virulent and culpable. For example, the inexcusable attacks on Ezra Pound and the modern poets in the middlebrow literary reviews have done much to stir up hatreds and nothing to enhance the possibility of a various and vital culture. When Elvis Presley says, as he did in supporting Stevenson for president, "I don't dig the intellectual bit," I don't get angry. But I do when a middlebrow intellectual says the same thing in more tiresome language.

GEORGE: You say the highbrows are admitted intellectuals and that the middlebrows are intellectual anti-intellectuals. I take it lowbrows are nonintellectual anti-intellectuals.

RALPH: Yes, that is the crude but necessary formula, since for better or worse this is the way Americans tend to define themselves.

GEORGE: But if you were a sociologist, your approach to these matters would be less tendentious and polemical?

RALPH: Certainly. I would try to emulate the method of David Riesman or someone like Russell Lynes and look at the manners and morals of America as if I were a visiting anthropologist from another culture. I would not stress cultural ideology, and in making categories, I would be less interested in what people assert and more in what their behavior shows them to be. What interests the critic, as opposed to the impartial observer, is the clash of ideas and the conflict of cultural attitudes. It is his job to sort these out and evaluate them. He cannot afford, like the impartial observer, to leave his own opinions in doubt and his prejudices unadmitted and unexplained. I follow Van Wyck Brooks in my use of terms. But as I have said, it strikes me that although his cultural analysis was right, his prescription for improvement was wrong.

GEORGE: I see—and you admit a possible prejudice in yourself?

RALPH: My impulse is always to defend the highbrow and the lowbrow against the middlebrow; this may be partly prejudice. As for my *position*, I try to be a no-brow. I think it's everybody's duty these days to look for radical values wherever they may appear on the cultural spectrum.

GEORGE: A final question about the "brow" terms. Besides the reasons you have already given, what is the advantage of using these terms as intellectual, rather than objective sociological categories? Of course I'm aware that even as you use them, they contain a large sociological element.

RALPH: The advantage is that they become dynamic and consequential ideas rather than inert and noncommittal descriptions. The writers and critics of the last decade have contented themselves with an unprecedentedly minute sociologizing. They have told us much that is new and important. But they have written in a deliberately noncommittal if not actually complacent way, as if they had no stake in our culture and no duty to guide or modify it. As critics they have not had the accent of greatness. They have lost the American spirit of radical prophecy and affirmation, as well as the spirit of critical pessimism. It is time to supplement mere sociologizing with a criticism that may lead to political-cultural action.

I am struck by how intellectually helpless and historically shortsighted are the critics who have been immersing themselves in sociology. It seems to me that they have become entranced by the sheer wilderness of facts and alleged facts that have been assembled. It is no paradox to say that they know too much about

America, more than they or we need to know or have use for. Furthermore the social critics who used to study politics and economics but now study sociology tend to derive their values from their image of the great, always self-renewing middle class. They view this class, with-its magical, if elusive and undefinable "mobility," as the matrix of society, in which all the contradictions, inequities, and conflicts are assuaged and mediated. They have become obsessed with this archetype of the mystic center.

To sum up, in two or more decades of introspection and sociological inquiry we have forgotten that the radical ideas of democracy, as well as scientific and literary ideas, must be granted a measure of intellectual autonomy and respect if they are to be made effective in our lives. It has become the custom to ask, not "Is this or that idea right or wrong?" but "What will happen to me, what will it reveal about me, where will it place me, if I profess it?" We have saturated and obscured ideas with psychiatric and sociological symbolisms.

As for the "brow" terms, as Brooks used them they were recognized as referring to different forms of cultural animus, but more important, they were seen to be intellectual categories and were used with a polemical and reformist intent. The social inquirers of more recent times, being interested only in cultural symbols, have performed a deintellectualization of these, as of all other categories. To put it another way, as Brooks used the term "highbrow," it meant basically "an intellectual"; as more recent writers use it, it means basically "a snob" or a member of an "elite." This blotting out of intellectual qualities, this castration of effective ideas by prestige values and consumption tastes and by the mystique of cultural power is at the root of our failure of mind.

But now let us return to our discussion of contradictions in American literature. . . .

GEORGE: I'm wondering if you have a place in your scheme for Hart Crane's symbol of connection—the bridge?

RALPH: Yes, Crane is all the more relevant because *The Bridge* is very much devoted to following Brooks' and Waldo Frank's program for the "rediscovery of America," for finding the "usable past" and the "focal point" of our culture. Thus one must pose the ever-instructive example of Crane's poem against Brooks' idea that America's writers and thinkers should take the middle way in search of an organic, whole, and self-contained image of their country. Great and moving as *The Bridge* is in some of its parts, the symbolism conspicuously fails to connect and unify the polarities and anomalies of which Crane is so acutely aware— aware even to the point of madness. It is true of course that locally in the poem the leading symbol does establish significant relationships. But everyone can see the failure of *The Bridge* to marshal itself into a coherent myth or epic poem which expresses the essence of American culture.

Even in his relaxed and informal moments, Crane did not rest easily in his sense of being a "middlebrow." In one of his letters to Gorham Munson, he has been speaking of Matthew Josephson and Sherwood Anderson, and he goes on to say that the two are "opposite poles. J. classic, hard and glossy—Anderson, crowd-bound, with the smell of the sod about him, uncouth. Somewhere between them is Hart Crane with a kind of wistful indetermination, still much puzzled." The sense of in-betweenness, doubtless reinforced in Crane by his homosexuality, was anything but "wistful" when the pressure of a passionate imagination brought it to expression, and Crane's "indetermination" frayed out into a more or less nihilistic mysticism in *The Bridge*, as he himself came sadly to admit. We are left, at the end of the poem, with the unhappy sense of the unnatural and willful strain of a mind bent on reconciling what, more properly considered, must have appeared to be eternal irreconcilables.

But now let me draw to a conclusion, before I have irretrievably bored you. First, the misleading English analogy, from which Americans have not yet freed themselves. In *America's Coming-of-Age* Brooks was in part misled by his idea of the English literary and intellectual state of mind—"the open, skeptical, sympathetic centrality" which "articulates the whole life of the people." No doubt this is a fair description of the admirable English habit of mind at its best. But in America, "centrality" is far more likely to smother and obscure openness, skepticism, and sympathy than to enhance them. The fact is that for a thousand years England has been engaged in creating the only great middlebrow culture in history, with its special skill (so incalculably valuable in political history) of compromise, finding the middle way, and making even its incorrigible eccentricities normative. Yet the most interesting modern American writers—Frank Norris and Stephen Crane, Ezra Pound, Hemingway, and Faulkner—have turned, not to English literary models, but to Russian, French, and Irish.

As I suggested a minute ago, the first consistent attempt in this country to create a consciously middlebrow literary taste was not that of Brooks but that of William Dean Howells, who, as is often said, was the mediator between two writers of greater genius than his own, Henry James and Mark Twain. Howells wanted to square American taste with the literature of centrality and moderation (and among his favorite writers were Tolstoy, Fielding, Jane Austen, George

Eliot, and Matthew Arnold). Yet he always half suspected and feared the truth: namely, that the American imagination was not destined to derive its life from
centrality and moderation but from alienation, separa-
tion, and extremity, and that its characteristic expression was to consist in sustained contraries. What Howells feared has turned out to have been true all along.
The real affinity of American literature is not with the
moderate authors Howells felt at home with, but with
Dostoievski and Balzac, Flaubert, and Zola, Nietzsche,
Rimbaud, and Joyce. Yet middlebrows see in American
culture only what is consonant with English culture.
They do not like or know American culture in its ex-
tremer aspects.

One must conclude, then, that although middlebrowism has won the day—whether permanently or
not who shall say?—the culture it has created has
turned out to be on the whole mediocre and dull, a
culture that has conspicuously failed to embody the
"exhilarating sense of conflict" and the prophetic crea-
tiveness Brooks looked forward to in *America's Coming-of-Age*. Brooks' essay is a great piece of writing,
but we have lived through enough history now to see
its fundamental error—namely, the idea that the duty
of the intelligentsia is to create and defend a middle
culture. It is the duty of the intelligentsia to learn to
be at ease with the extremities of our culture and to
exult in the dialectic agility which seeks out and cham-
pions radical values no matter where they are found.

GEORGE: And you think that readers in general have
lost sight of these radical values?

RALPH: Nothing could be plainer. Let me provisionally limit what you call "readers in general" to those
who follow the lead of (1) the older generation of professors of American literature and (2) the critics of our
day.

The opinions of my esteemed academic colleagues may be found, in all their rhetorical vagueness and with full middlebrow bravura, in the official monstrosity known as *Literary History of the United States,* an estimable production that for ten years now has been heralded in bad grammar and shaky metaphor as the last word on the subject. It is of some cultural interest to compare this production with the earlier official history—*The Cambridge History of American Literature.* The earlier work was, by modern standards, full of factual error and aberrant judgment; yet it was a generally humane work, in which one felt the invigoratingly discordant voices of the many contributors. It was a many-volumed book written by different men with different temperaments, styles, and opinions. But the editors of *Literary History* tried, by a system of what they called "group conferences," to achieve uniformity, to "relate" the contributions "to one another within a frame." One result of this attempt is a kind of impersonal, anonymous style, with occasional spurts of ecstasy and uplift, and much bureaucratic jargon. Another result is that the moral tone is that of a group conference—perfectly free, that is, of individual accent or conviction or wit. There is much corporate benevolence, and there are many affirmations about the international function of American literature. The editors tend to regard the great writers of the past as consciously contributing to a group project sanctioned by the values of a culture which is liberal in politics and conservative-middlebrow in taste. Of course there is much sound, solid stuff in *Literary History,* and it is unfair to quote out of context. Nevertheless, there are some sentences from the chapter on "Folklore" which I have never forgotten, so clear a vista do they seem to open upon the technological future. "Phonograph, radio, and sound movie now expand indefinitely the range of oral transmission. At the same time, with universally accessible print intelligible to a literate people, they diminish the need for memory. Folklore may instantly become literature, and literature may speedily travel the road to folklore. Their interaction . . . will be beneficial to both." So you see, George, we don't have to worry any more about the inefficient and outmoded thing called "memory."

GEORGE: Why stop at memory? Can't we also get rid of some of the troublesome kindred activities of the mind, like imagination and consecutive reasoning?

RALPH: Why indeed? I see you have no more liking than I for the moral style of technology and bureaucracy as they bear upon literary studies. It is sad that so many literary professors have become indistinguishable from clerks, statisticians, and positive thinkers. In the last fifteen years they have edited and bibliographed American literature to a fare-thee-well. In teaching, they inevitably picture the great writers of the past as tame and cooperative persons like themselves.

GEORGE: It is no surprise that their students should lose sight of what you call the radical values of American literature. But what about the young people who have followed the critics rather than the scholars?

RALPH: It may be said for them that they have been reading the great novels and poems assiduously. But on the whole, they have been looking for only two things—either technical brilliance, the adroit use of language and metaphor, myth, and symbol, or, moral exempla that lend significance to the daily perplexities of the life of the family and of the community. Although the earnest and shortsighted readers of our time have found something of what they looked for, they have acquired a new dissatisfaction with American literature and a feeling of alienation from it. They find technical brilliance among the romancers such as Melville, Hawthorne, Poe, and Faulkner, but although they purport to discover universal moral values in these writers, often of a religious and conservative order, they tend to reject these writers on the grounds that they are insufficiently aware of manners and morals, of the ordinary life of man in society. On the other hand, the earnest but shortsighted reader admits that our naturalist and realist writers, like Norris, Dreiser, O'Neill, Dos Passos, Farrell, Anderson, and Lewis, have something to tell us about the life of man in society, but he discounts them because of their stylistic clumsiness, falsity, or vulgarity. Only one writer has pleased everyone, by meeting all the standard requirements of the modern reader—Henry James. Now, James is my idea of a very great writer; he was American to the core. Yet of how much in American life he was ignorant! And how mistaken it is to judge all of our writers by their proximity to or departure from the practice and precept of James!

GEORGE: I don't think James was ignorant of life—of America or politics or sex. He knew all there is to know, although there is much that he prefers to communicate by ambiguous intimation. . . . But you have been using the phrase "radical values." What does it mean?

RALPH: First, the virtue of truth-telling, the determination to find out the really controlling facts and principles on which our society operates. Second, the liberal heritage of the Renaissance and the Enlightenment as this is given political expression in our Declaration of Independence and the Bill of Rights and cultural expression by our imaginative writers.

GEORGE: You spoke a minute ago of the "earnest and shortsighted reader." I'm afraid that's me. Suppose I become for the moment carefree and take the long view—what "larger significance" can I expect to see?

RALPH: That American literature is the utterance of
a democratic faith and the mirror of a democratic culture, that it finds truth and liberation in an imagined
world whose implications are individualistic rather
than corporate, political rather than religious, that it
exults in a world of experience that is felt to be open,
disruptive, skeptical, contradictory, novel, and emergent, that at its best it is adequately, though seldom
systematically, aware of fatality, evil, and human limitation, but that it does not draw its characteristic inspiration from the moral preoccupations that follow
from this awareness.

GEORGE: An admirable summary. I have one more
question. It occurs to me that the real danger to a vital
culture is not middlebrowism but the mass media. I
gather that you and Dorothy have no qualms about TV
and comic books for the children.

RALPH: Nor for ourselves. I consume a good deal of
both, because I like them and not out of a sociological
curiosity.

GEORGE: Well, I am not so sure. For the moment, at
least, we are not going to have TV. I feel a duty to
put a floor under our children's culture and keep the
influence of mass entertainment in the cellar. Don't you
think that TV entertainment, being a cliché art, is
deadening and inhibits discrimination and the development of the faculty of attention?

RALPH: Yes, no doubt a lot of it does, although some
of it is very good. I'd better not speak for myself, but
I can't see that it has hurt my children. Now that the
novelty has worn off, they look at TV only occasionally.
As for the question of the general effect of mass culture, this has been studied in all its perplexity by countless literary critics, psychiatrists, and sociologists. You
will perhaps think me misguided if I say that I am not
particularly worried about the effect of mass culture,

although it is certainly a formidable phenomenon. There is much vitality in it, especially in the movies and in jazz, and there is much that is tiresome and possibly dangerous to the spirit of man. But one can take it or leave it; it is there when one wants it. It is inevitable in a mass civilization and I doubt if the trailer-dwellers of Los Angeles or the workers of Detroit can be converted to folk song, legend-spinning, and ritual-dancing.

While the mass culture has been endlessly scrutinized and moralized upon and the highbrows have been endlessly needled and dissected, the middle culture has got off scot free, on the assumption that it constitutes the mainstream, which preserves all the great humanist values from the dangerous deviations of the highbrows and the lowbrows. Nevertheless, although the native dialectic is between the high and the low culture, the most fruitful *argument* in American culture is the one between the highbrow and the middlebrow, since lowbrowism by definition does not articulate, in the form of argument, its aspirations or its function.

It strikes me as obvious that in America the middle culture, as a significant and admirable human achievement, does not exist. Why, then, does it remain unchallenged in its privileged sanctuary of commercial success and academic respectability? This is the first question that needs to be raised if we are to have any sort of radical criticism in America.

But I see that whereas we were comfortably sitting in the shade an hour or so ago, we are now in the sun. It is going to be a warm day. What do you say to a swim in the pit before the mob returns.

GEORGE: Good idea. It may clear my brain. Right now I am overstimulated by the heady mixture of ideas you have been serving me. I am already in your debt for a state of mind which combines stupefaction and exhilaration in approximately equal degrees. I am afloat in a welter of brilliant *aperçus*, shifting lights and darks, disturbing insights, dubious abstractions, and probable errors. I feel as if I have been drinking.

RALPH: It is odd, but commendable, that you are intoxicated by the simple truths of a democratic civilization.

Saturday Afternoon:

The Still Point

As Ralph Headstrong picks his way along the ledges and clambers over the sea wall, fortunately not high at this point, he catches sight of Maggie Motive across the broad lawn. She is leaning over a flower garden at the front of the Motives' new and very expensive modern house, in the wide east windows of which Ralph momentarily notices that the sea and the sky are mirrored, behind the geraniums in the window boxes. Maggie is forty-eight and is a woman of projects and free-lance intellectual interests. Over the years she has been a painter of water colors and maker of ceramics, a geologist's assistant and mistress, a stage designer and factotum with a Federal Theater group, secretary and assistant editor of Harper's Bazaar, *hostess at the United Nations, and teacher of the modern novel in an Adult Education Course (in this last pursuit she was momentarily brilliant, as in everything she does, and succeeded in winning several students away from the courses in Canasta and Dog Obedience). Among her projects have been a number of men, including the two husbands she has divorced; these were a Chicago businessman and a highbrow critic who later became a writer of detective stories, until apparently overcome by remorse at having betrayed his position as an intellectual, he finally settled down to a morbid career of alcoholism and writing book reviews for the Sunday* Times. *Her present husband is a wealthy man of high principle and tiresome rhetoric—the executive secre-*

tary of the Magnanimous Philanthropical Fund. Hop-
ing that Albert Motive won't be present, Ralph hails
Maggie from a distance and gets a gay wave of the gar-
den shears, with which she is cutting zinnias. Among
all her bewildering careers, Ralph thinks, she has never
been able to make a career of herself, and thus there
is nothing sustained and cumulative about her—except
the legend, a dizzy farrago of fact and fiction, she
makes of her lengthening past. But she looks young and
attractive today in her loose yellow frock pulled in
tight at the waist. Her long hair, still naturally brown-
black, is piled rather precariously on top of her head.

MAGGIE: Come on in. On the back porch is the spray
gun and nicotine dust you asked to borrow. But don't
go now. Stay and keep me company. Dorothy and the
others will be over later for the drink I offered them,
won't they?

RALPH: As soon as Darlene, the baby-sitter, gets
back. Darlene wants to be a model. She has been
photographed and interviewed by three agencies in
New York. This morning she received her plastic
smiling-teeth in the mail, and she has been allowed to
go to Gloucester alone to show them to some friends.
She is fifteen, but very mature.

MAGGIE: I can imagine. (*Arranging the zinnias in a*
vase.) My husband has gone off to Martha's Vineyard
to a convention of Foundation executives. They are
planning to integrate their activities at the level of
group-cooperation. This would be tantamount to channeling different areas with respect to a Super-Founda-
tion which would facilitate formalization and activiza-
tion of those present aspects of Foundation procedure
which unsuccessfully seek to avoid overlapping and
multipurpose malfunctioning—at least I think that is

what Albert said. The word "tantamount" always makes me think of a fierce beast of the cat family.

RALPH: That's "catamount."

MAGGIE: Ah, well, don't destroy my illusions needlessly. Before he left this morning Albert received a special delivery letter from a man in California who wants financial assistance to complete the sixth and last canto of a 12,000-line poem in heroic couplets on the nature of tragedy. Of course the poor man hasn't got a chance, even though he may turn out to be another Horace or Boileau. He is not a group, and Foundations like groups, especially those seeking new means of manipulating the environment, both human and material. My notion of manipulating the environment is growing flowers, and getting people to do what I want them to do. Right now I want you to sit on the lawn with me and talk. I will show you that I am not so frivolous as you think.

RALPH: Talk about tragedy?

MAGGIE: Why not? I don't believe I could stand a discussion of tragedy from a *technical* point of view, as an art form. But it interests me as a cultural phenomenon. Isn't it true that tragedy is fashionable nowadays?

RALPH (*as they settle into the lawn chairs*): Yes, the tragic sense of life has been commended by intellectuals during the last fifteen years as never before. The general desire to have a tragic view of things is very strong among literary people, especially. For them tragedy is allied with myth and symbol.

MAGGIE: And myth and symbol too have been much talked about. What is your definition of tragedy?

RALPH: You are a genius at impromptu definition. What do you say?

MAGGIE: You asked for it. I think of tragedy as a kind of superior realism, an intense and profound acceptance of the sad facts of life. It gives us a heightened awareness of life, which does not inhibit, and in fact makes possible, morally significant acts. It alleviates our primitive and unreflective fears and purifies the pity we feel for our unhappy fellow men. My suspicion is, however, that for most people nowadays tragedy is a mode of transcendence and denial, rather than a mode of reattachment to the world we live in.

RALPH: Good. There is no doubt that many people confuse tragedy with religion, preferring, for example, *Oedipus at Colonus* to *Oedipus the King* because in the former the hero's divine transcendence occurs, whereas in the latter he is entangled with the problems of the real world. They see in the tragic catharsis a reconciliation of contradictions analogous to the Christian incarnation. For others, like our new friend George, the important thing about the tragic view is what you call its heightened awareness of life and its preparation of the individual for morally significant action. Still, I think of George as wishing to embody tragedy without the tragic stress and agony, and as wishing to embody comedy without the comic *esprit*, and the health-giving gaiety. It may turn out that the submerged lifestyle of the Americans of the future will be a higher style of tragedy and comedy. Will our descendants make the grade? George thinks so, but he is young and an optimist.

MAGGIE: I would say that the general tone of life in America has had the thinness, the instability, and flashy brilliance of melodrama and farce, rather than of tragedy and comedy. That is my sense of our literature, my sense of Mark Twain, Melville, Hawthorne, and Whitman—my sense and Constance Rourke's. But I like it that way, although I don't know that I could say offhand what are the virtues of a melodramatic view of things.

RALPH: Quite apart from the notorious faults of melodrama, such as sensationalism and sentimentality, it has the great virtue of presenting an open, skeptical, disruptive world in which, though values may be over-simplified, they are clear. It does not pretend to reconcile contradictions; it is content to rest among them. I think this is the state of mind the critic and general observer needs to get himself into today. At least I get into this state of mind whenever I hear people talk in hushed and reverential tones about the tragic view, as if it were something one surrenders to, falls back on with a sigh of relief, rather than something one wins in agony and suffering. One cannot swoon into great-ness, and that is what people are trying to do—swoon, that is, into tragedy and the tragic sense of life.

MAGGIE: What is behind the modern literary con-cern with tragedy, myth, and symbol—I mean in its merely modish and temporary, not in its truly serious form?

RALPH: The same impulse that is behind modern mediocrity and conformity—the search for a mystic center which will alleviate contradictions and which will absorb and annihilate the conscious self, thus quell-ing the self's spirit of adventure and the pain and trav-ail of the self as it seeks to work out its destiny in an intractable world. This image of rest and centrality is the mystic rose of the contemporary quest. Of course it takes many different forms, varying in sophistication and profundity, as well as in meaning and context— from the middle-of-the-wayism of the political liberals to "the still point of the turning world" and the pool with the lotus flower Mr. Eliot searches for in his "Quartets." And Yeats, in the most famous lines of verse in modern times, appears to exhort us to take up the search:

Turning and turning in the widening gyre
The falcon cannot hear the falconer;
Things fall apart; the centre cannot hold;
Mere anarchy is loosed upon the world . . .

MAGGIE: Do you claim that falcons should not hear falconers?

RALPH: It depends on what the falcon is up to and who the falconer is and what he is saying—and whether he exists. Yeats' lines should be taken seriously in so far as they urge us to achieve political stability in the world. But this does not prove that the idea of centrality is valid or useful in aesthetic or cultural matters.

MAGGIE: As I understand them, the modern theories of the derivation of tragedy and of myth are the same.

RALPH: Well, tragedy derives from the Dionysian rites, the ritual of the death and rebirth of the young hero-god. Of course, as Gilbert Murray and others have pointed out, the Greek plays often seem to mirror this ritual. And not only the tragic plays, but those of Aristophanes too. Francis Fergusson's *Idea of a Theater* follows in general the interpretation of tragedy we are discussing. It is perhaps the only distinguished work of literary criticism which does so.

MAGGIE: I've looked into some of those people one is supposed to know about—Murray, Jane Harrison, Frazer and his *Golden Bough*, Lord Raglan. I even read a touching and delirious book by Joseph Campbell, called *The Hero with a Thousand Faces*.

RALPH: Most impressive. Have you derived a generalization from these writers?

MAGGIE: That myth, like tragedy, derives from the ritual of the dying god, Adonis, Osiris, Christ, and all the rest—or rather that this is the interpretation agreed on by most of the mythologists and literary critics.

RALPH: That is the modern interpretation of myth,

the one, that is, that has taken hold. It should be said
immediately, however, that there is much evidence to
refute this interpretation, in so far as it purports to explain more than the limited body of myth to which it
is actually applicable. It cannot explain *all* myths by
any means. The American anthropologists, having
rather too little taste for literature and the imagination,
and themselves writing rather badly, disappoint us
when we turn to them in order to learn about myth.
They do not like to generalize on their findings. Still,
they have much to tell us. I am referring to people like
Ruth Benedict, Franz Boas, and Paul Radin. These anthropologists don't accept the dying-god theory, and,
although, as I say, they are wary of all generalizations,
they include in their books a good deal of evidence
bearing on the origin and meaning of myth which it
is impossible to reconcile with the dying-god interpretation. Their assumption always is that myth is a form
of imaginative literature emerging in various ways
from the context of tribal tradition, folklore, and magic
which it mirrors, explains, and reaffirms.

As for the persistent attempt of the theorists to re-
duce myth to a single origin and meaning, the usual
reply of the American anthropologists is that of Miss
Benedict, who thought it ironic that scholars and critics
(I think I recall the passage correctly) should have
labored so persistently "under the incubus of theories
explaining seven-headed monsters and magic swords
as survivals of primordial conditions, allegories of the
sun and moon or of the sex act, or etiological philoso-
phizing and have ignored the unconfined role of the
human imagination in the creation of mythology." The
myth critics of our time—I mean those critics loosely
and often inaccurately associated with the New Criticism—object to Miss Benedict's idea of an unconfined
imagination. It rubs them the wrong way. They love a

simplified and dogmatic idea of myth, especially one which connects literature with religious ritual.

MAGGIE: It is certain that the religious impulse is strongly felt by many of the mythologists and critics I have read. They find in the notion of the dying god either a sanction for their religious faith or a substitute for the faith they would like to have but don't.

RALPH: True enough. And the death and rebirth motif satisfies many other cravings too. Its manifold cultural significance is truly extraordinary, and very much worth investigating. For literary people especially, but also for thousands, millions of others, it is by all odds the most influential of ideas. One might almost call it the archetype of the modern mind. Its being the theory of the myth critics is only one aspect of its influence.

MAGGIE: Supposing you are right, my inclination is to ascribe this to a general anxiety, weariness, and apathy, to a thorough disillusion with the radical human values that came down to us from the Renaissance and the Enlightenment. Does that make sense? This is indeed an afternoon devoted to delightful generalizations. Have you any more?

RALPH: I have one that merely elaborates what you just said. The hold on men's minds exerted by the death and rebirth myth suggests that they are weary of the idea of the self—the self, that is, conceived as an entity created and defined by the human organism in interaction with the circumstances of its real, its mundane condition. It is true that some writers present myth as a way of achieving selfhood, a superior way. For example, a prophetic moralist like your Joseph Campbell presents myth as a way of shuffling off the mundane self and achieving a transfigured self. He believes (doesn't he?) that myth is a superior kind of wisdom which came naturally to the happier folk of primeval eras—a form of wisdom which we must re-capture if we are to be saved. But so far as I can make out from his book, the transfigured self is a terribly vague and mystical sort of thing, ill-equipped to deal with the problems of the world, and not at all equipped for its pleasures.

MAGGIE: Can you confirm my impression that older interpretations of myth described it as an expression of man's struggle to survive, and to understand the world rather than to escape from it?

RALPH: Yes. Although there have been many theories about myth, the general tendency from the Renaissance down to very recent decades was to think of myth as an expression of the will to live in and to know this world. Now it is thought of as expressing a spiritual crisis or *agon,* the first symbolic act of which is to die. The second act is the rebirth, the transfigured life. But the quality and significance of this transfiguration remain unclear to me—I am not prepared for this release of the self into the Unknown; I like to be encompassed by reality, or what I take to be reality. I quake at the modern will to self-annihilation—immersion in the destructive element, as Conrad says.

MAGGIE: I admire your strength of mind. But as I look out into the abyss of the sea, I seem to feel a harsh rigidity in your aloofness from the mysteries of the unconscious and of the gods in their hidden beauty and power. I believe I would feel easier about you if you could relax upon the dusky bosom of our Great Mother and heave a guiltless sigh. What would life be like, I wonder, without some connection with the mysteries, without a simple piety to the hidden sources of our being. However, my mask of the afternoon is the physiognomy of Enlightenment. I am determined to be as rational as Diderot's Mlle. de l'Espinasse.

RALPH: Ah, *there* was a woman.

MAGGIE: It occurs to me that all the talk I hear from literary people about "the initiation theme" is connected with the cult of the dying god. In the so-called *rites de passage,* the childish self dies and the adult self is born. This psychic and spiritual change is thought of as a magical mutation rather than as a continuous development.

RALPH: Yes, this sort of thinking has given a new tone to discussions of America's most famous possession: its innocence. Graduate students assiduously discover the theme of initiation in *Huckleberry Finn,* in *The Red Badge of Courage,* in *Moby Dick,* in James' *The American,* and *The Ambassadors,* and so on. Generally speaking, you see, it is a question of the young or innocent American being initiated into life in the wilderness (Hemingway's *In Our Time*), in war (*The Red Badge*), or in Europe (James' novels). The neophyte is a fragmented and incomplete personality until his ordeal has made him whole, given him new life, and——

MAGGIE: Rendered him indistinguishable from the people in Arthurian romance—Sir Gawain, grail quests, perilous chapels, and so on.

RALPH: Too true. Outside of two or three stories, like Cooper's *Deerslayer* and Faulkner's *The Bear,* there are no sustained myths of initiation or of transfiguration in American literature. The typical American hero is not susceptible to a spiritual *agon.* He is aloof and stoical. He looks at life coldly and unflinchingly, though perhaps ignorantly. He may learn things, he may change his moral opinions; but at the end of the book he will be, spiritually, pretty much where he was at the beginning—Huck Finn, Christopher Newman, Lambert Strether, Frederic Henry, *et al.* The American hero, if I may posit him for a moment, moves in accordance with a sort of irresolute destiny, among the contradictions and imperfections of his world. He does not imagine a transcendent ground of being, where contradictions are reconciled and imperfections perfected. He lives with his own inner contradictions; he does not believe that these are to be escaped or harmonized by a spiritual transfiguration. At best he is a melodramatist, a humorist—at worst, a fatalist.

MAGGIE: To return to our general point, you think that the people who see initiation themes and death and rebirth myths everywhere are fearful of experience and its anomalies? They find these myths attractive because they have lost their faith in rational inquiry and in skeptical criticism?

RALPH: It is as plain as day.

MAGGIE: I don't keep up with the literary quarterlies, but it seems to me that in the interest of completeness we have got to include the symbolist critics along with the myth critics. As I understand the people who write in the general spirit of Cassirer and Mrs. Langer, they see in the process of literary creation a myth of death and rebirth. That is, what happens during the process by which a poem comes into being is that reality and the dialectical modes of understanding reality die and are reborn in the symbol, the symbol then being taken for a higher reality and a form of superior knowledge. One of these critics says, if I remember correctly, that the poetic symbol is "the incarnation of meaning." The symbol is an autonomous unity, irreversibly transfigured from reality. It absorbs and reconciles all the contradictions that confront us as the mind contemplates reality. All the dualistic verities of Western thought are thus mysteriously disposed of and all orders of meaning are swallowed up by language, by the omnivorous, predatory symbol. Literature reflects neither the mind and emotions of its creator nor external reality. It looks forward, rather, to the symbolic form in which, once this form is achieved, the author's mind and emotions and his sense of reality will have been annihilated.

RALPH: A very accurate account. It is a corollary of the symbolist critic, is it not, that the subject matter of the literary work is always the process by which it achieved symbolic form? The subject of literature is literature; it is like the snake swallowing its tail.

MAGGIE: Well, the symbolist critics are certainly not read by many people. It occurs to me, however, that Toynbee's *Study of History* is widely read and that his theory of history is allied to what we are talking about. All that about "withdrawal" and "return," transfiguration and the new life, etc. For the older theories of history—such as the environmental, the economic, and the evolutionary—he has substituted the myth of the dying god.

RALPH: You are a student of Toynbee? Indeed you are a prodigious scholar.

MAGGIE: My husband's book club sent the one-volume *Study*. I browsed enough to discover that Toynbee believes in the *elite* theory of history. He says that civilizations are led "upward" by gifted individuals who form a creative minority—a sort of avant-garde. This vanguard does not, according to Toynbee, rule by force while a civilization is still growing; it persuades the masses by "charm" and unconscious suggestion. The creative minority are those who can mystically relive in their souls the death and resurrection of the divine hero. They, and the civilization they lead, attain their goal by "the movement of Withdrawal-and-Return." They withdraw from the world, that is, when some great task faces them; in the privacy of the spirit they prepare themselves to return reborn to the world and take up the challenge.

RALPH: So that, for example, Lenin's residence in

Switzerland during the years before 1917 was a mystical withdrawal and preparation of spirit, rather than, as one had thought, a tactic of revolution and an escape from the Tsar's police?

MAGGIE: Yes. Toynbee makes of history a myth or tragedy, in the sense in which we have been using these words. But a civilization may withdraw and return, as it were, in the right way or the wrong way. The right way is Christian, the wrong, pagan. The Indians once failed in the person of Buddha, who dissolved himself in Nirvana. The Greeks failed in the person of Plato, who withdrew but did not return to the world. The Romans failed in the person of Marcus Aurelius, who lost himself in the mystic City of Zeus. These men were annihilated in the mystic experience —dismembered like the Greek god of the tragedies in his *sparagmos;* the Christian heroes of history, on the other hand, have returned from death transfigured, and have led society toward God.

RALPH: These fancies make a sort of Sargasso Sea for the beguiled reader to float about in.

MAGGIE: Yes, Toynbee's theory seems to be a great mystery and consolation. Actually, though, it may be a form of elaborate and grandiose mystification rather than a profound mystery. True, he makes one thing clear enough—he has a romantic love of doom and annihilation. He predicts the imminent wreck of Western civilization not with horror but with a grim and gloating pleasure.

RALPH: Do you suppose it is this specious mysticism and glib familiarity with doom that has made so many people think of Toynbee as a Guiding Light?

MAGGIE: Probably. It would seem that many people nowadays are secretly discouraged and feel self-pity. Perhaps these people like to fancy themselves as the suffering protagonist in the drama of history—the protagonist who, as Toynbee says, is "scourged, racked, shackled, blinded with hot irons and put to every torment" but through whose agony mankind mounts one more step in its weary ascent to the ultimate Community of Saints. Also, Toynbee is a terrible culture-monger and Heavy Thinker. Instead of saying that people don't want to face reality, he calls them "Do-asyoulikes" and says they are attracted by the "temptations of Odysseus" and "the flesh pots of Egypt." Chiding the modern skeptic, Toynbee calls him the "graceless *Homo Occidentalis* who has turned against the Christianity that found him a barbarian and has promoted him to the lordship of creation."

RALPH: That is very grandiloquent.

MAGGIE: Toynbee's *History* is as good as a TV quiz show or Bartlett's *Quotations*. You are likely to find on a single page quotations from A. E. Housman, Heraclitus, Whitman, Gerald Heard, Job, Lucretius, and Field Marshal Smuts. The implication always is that these people are great authorities on world history.

RALPH: Toynbee allots to them a vast amount of unaccredited wisdom—to himself also.

MAGGIE: Yes, it is Superior Wisdom, not common-sense wisdom. You have read Joseph Campbell's *The Hero with a Thousand Faces?* I wouldn't mention it except for Campbell's remarkable Mr. So-and-so, one of the most depressing characters of modern times. The book is full of fascinating lore. But before long I got swamped by heroes: the serpent Kheti, Sargon, Ishtar, Jesus, Conchobar, Blood Clot Boy, and so on and so forth. I also got swamped by language. There is resounding Toynbeean-Biblical language ("And where we had thought to find an abomination, we shall find a god . . . where we had thought to be alone, we shall be with all the world"); there is Joycean wordplay ("Full circle, from the tomb of the womb to the womb

of the tomb, we come"), and there is even, it seems, the
language of Thurber ("No man can return from such
[spiritual] exercises and take very seriously himself as
Mr. So-and-so of Such-and-such a township, U. S. A.—
Society and duties drop away. Mr. So-and-so, having
discovered himself big with man, becomes indrawn
and aloof").

RALPH: Do you gather that Mr. So-and-so is in-
tended to strike us as comical?

MAGGIE: It is impossible to tell. Since the author has
never established in the book his own voice and point
of view, we have no means of comparison. However,
the meaning is clear. Mr. So-and-so is the *homme
moyen sensuel,* the ordinary man as ordinary man.
Mr. Campbell believes that what is wrong with this ordinary man is that he is a bad case of rampant self-
development. Mr. Campbell admonishes us to stop being individuals. He says that in the past, when the great
mythologies flourished, "all meaning was in the group,
in the anonymous forms, none in the self-expressive individual; today no meaning is in the group—none in
the world: all is in the individual." Can you imagine a
more erroneous statement about the modern world? It
would hardly be worth noticing, except that so many
other modern thinkers say that the idea of the self is
reprehensible and that the self must be extinguished in
the name of salvation or of art or of history or of the
state or of the community.

RALPH: Don't you think, by the way, that for some
writers, myth became in the 1940's and '50's a substitute for the Stalinism on which they had in part been
brought up but which they could no longer accept?
Perhaps we can say that in the 1930's Mr. So-and-so
became indrawn and aloof when he felt himself big
with the proletarian cause. He was got with child, that
is, by the proletariat rather than by Universal Man,

or whoever it is that has been making love to Mr. Campbell's So-and-so.

MAGGIE: Enough of these monstrosities. I cannot endure them. . . . I haven't read *Finnegans Wake,* but doesn't that come in here somewhere?

RALPH: Yes, the idea of myth in Joyce's symptomatic book is generally the one we have been discussing. The story, if such it may be called, is based on a comic song about the apparent death and resurrection of an Irish workman. Somewhere in the book the author observes that it is "strangely cult for this ceasing of the yore." And before he gets through, Joyce has identified his hero, Earwicker, with all sorts of fertility cults and with Osiris, Attis, Adonis, Balder, Dionysus, Christ, and any number of absurd Peruvian and Ojibway deities. At the same time, there is an implied Freudian interpretation, which appeals to me more. There is a good deal about the "family umbroglio"—we are supposed to think not only of the family umbrella but of the Oedipal conflict with its attendant neuroses and the myths that express them. Earwicker is called a "neuropean."

MAGGIE: Is he Mr. So-and-so?

RALPH: Certainly. He is the ordinary man. But the most interesting parts of *Finnegans Wake* are those in which we are able to think of Earwicker, however remotely, as an individual living in Dublin with his family and having certain daily adventures. Unhappily, the hero gets smothered by Joyce's erudition and his mystic abstractions and allusions. As R. G. Davis has said, *Finnegans Wake* is the culmination of the modern mythic movement in literature. It is also its *reductio ad absurdum.* Still, it is a great work after all.

MAGGIE: I incline to agree that Freud has much to tell us about myth, beyond the obvious, and therefore tiresome, symbols of flagpoles and—oceans. *Moses and Monotheism* is the only psychoanalytic book I have ever read, but it excited me very much. But what about Jung and the "archetype" criticism that literary critics have based on his psychology?

RALPH: I feel that this criticism is of little use. It applies as well to *Li'l Abner* as to the *Divine Comedy* and with the same results. Being absorbed in "archetypes," the critic loses all sense of particularities and differences, of context and history. Personality, in the author of a novel or poem as well as in the characters he has created, is effaced by being universalized according to type.

MAGGIE: Everyone is turned into the detestable Mr. So-and-so?

RALPH: Exactly. . . . May I have a drink?

MAGGIE: Not until you have summed up what we have said, and added a necessary caveat.

RALPH: We have looked into some of the more recondite but characteristic contemporary modes of literary and quasi-religious opinion. We have found there a leading archetype of the time—a symbolic action of the spirit, which we have called variously death and resurrection, the ritual of initiation, withdrawal and return. We have admitted that in some ways there is a possibility in modern thought of a new profundity of tragic or religious understanding. We have shown, however, that generally speaking the more recondite moderns, who spurn the philistines and middlebrows, are really moved in the same way they are—namely, by a desire, not for real spiritual insight and transcendence, or for the illumination that may come of struggle and suffering, but for a mystical centrality of taste and opinion and emotion, for the feeling of tensions untensed, of the will relaxed, of dynamism stilled, of contradictions resolved, of tranquillity achieved and pain avoided.

MAGGIE: And the caveat?

RALPH: I don't know. Should there be one?

MAGGIE: Yes. It is probable that we have proceeded too much by free association and have failed to demonstrate that all the kinds of centrality of which we have spoken can be logically associated or that there are significant analogies among them.

RALPH: Well, let us cling, nevertheless, to our generalizations and assume, until we are argued out of them, that they refer with sufficient accuracy to at least some of the complicated cultural realities of our day. Let us suppose, at the very least, that they are valid as a critical point of view, a provisional mode of investigation.

MAGGIE: Agreed.

RALPH (*looking furtively at Maggie, but assuming a light and off-hand air*): As for myth, no doubt Robert Graves is right. All myth and poetry derive from the White Goddess. Do you recall his poem about her?

> All saints revile her, and all sober men
> Ruled by the God Apollo's golden mean—
> In scorn of which we sailed to find her
> In distant regions likeliest to hold her
> Whom we desired above all things to know,
> Sister of the mirage and echo. . . .

MAGGIE: Yes, I remember it now. Please don't continue. There are some improper expressions in the next two stanzas and I know that in pronouncing them you would not merely be claiming the right to free discourse between enlightened persons; you would also be making love to me. Furthermore, I should know that you were making love to me—because you would be presenting a view of myth which I accept but which I know you do not. However, I join you in scorning saints, sober men, and golden means. And now I shall get you a drink.

RALPH (*coldly*): Thank you. It will be necessary to

get several. Dorothy and the Middlebys are at the sea wall. They have had six children on their hands all afternoon at the beach. They will need a drink.

Later, the Headstrongs, the Middlebys, and Maggie are sitting on the terrace to the landward of the house. The terrace is covered on top and the two sides with open latticework of a particularly graceful redwood design. On the light green benches at the sides and back are Maggie's red and yellow tuberous begonias; obviously they have been a big success this year. The floor is of flagstone, and the persons of the scene sit around a large circular ironwork table painted white, with a glass top. The chairs, too, are of white iron. The martinis which Maggie has delegated George to make are extremely refreshing, yet to her taste there is too much vermouth. George has made them one-to-four, explaining that the tide within the martini glass has begun to turn in favor of vermouth and predicting, to Maggie's horror, that a one-to-one formula will be the accepted thing in the back yards and rumpus rooms of the suburbs within five years.

DOROTHY (*who seems only somewhat refreshed by the afternoon at the beach*): I am afraid we cannot stay long; the children must be fed. But I want to know what you two intellectuals have been talking about. At the beach, we were trying to arrive at some agreement about psychoanalysis and what has happened to it in America since Freud. But Genevieve kept getting sand in her eyes, Herman took off his trunks because he had an erection, Ellen floated on her inner tube around the rocks at the end of the beach heading for Ireland and had to be rescued by a boy in a hot-rod outboard, and Bobby amused himself by pinching the backs of fat ladies. Consequently our discussion didn't get far.

RALPH (*irrelevantly*): Soon one more item of American culture will have disappeared—the patched inner tube kids swim on. *All* future tires will be tubeless. Lewis & Conger will sell plastic imitations of inner tubes at $49.50 each. When I was a child——

MAGGIE: We have been talking about myths and middlebrows, tragedy and the state of the modern soul. I would like to hear what you have to say about psychiatry. I am ignorant about it, yet I would sooner die than take to the couch. I have always prided myself on my resolve to take to the couch only for nonpsychiatric purposes. I do not want anyone rummaging around in my unconscious, especially for fifty dollars an hour—that is, unless they pay *me*. I imagine my views may be retrograde, although I'll make a guess that Ralph shares them.

RALPH: I do. Still, whether to be analyzed or not must always be a question for the individual.

DOROTHY: I know how Maggie feels. Yet surely, psychiatry has become an integral part of modern life. We all show its effects in one way or another. Don't you agree, George?

GEORGE (*eager to have his say*): Absolutely. By the way, a story told by the Winnebago Indians occurs to me. It seems to make a connection between myth and psychiatry. May I tell it?

ALL: Please do.

GEORGE: I learned it from Paul Radin's book called *Winnebago Hero Cycles*. Mr. Radin collected the tales which are the basis of his book from the Winnebago raconteur Sam Blowsnake. They have to do with a progression from anarchy to culture that reminds Radin of Aeschylus and a progression from the infantile self to the adult self that reminds him of Rabelais and Freud.

The four cycles tell the stories of Trickster, Hare,

Red Horn, and the Twins. In the first episode of the
Trickster cycle, Trickster, the chief of the tribe, enter-
tains his companions at a warbundle feast preparatory
to going on the warpath. But instead of going on the
warpath he rudely leaves before the feast is over in
order to cohabit with a woman. This procedure is repeated three times and was presumably a matter of
great charm and interest to the Winnebagos who heard
the tale told, not only because of its sheer humorous
perversity, but because Trickster was violating two
cardinal Winnebago rules: the chief does not himself
go on the warpath and those who do must never cohabit with a woman before going. In succeeding epi-
sodes Trickster stands by while his left arm gets into a
fight with his right; he borrows two children and allows
them to die; he burns his anus with a firebrand because, though he had commanded it to protect some
roasting ducks while he slept, it had failed; seeing a
man pointing across a pond, Trickster mimics him as
long as his muscles will allow and then perceives that
the pointing man is a stump; Trickster, who reminds
us first of Rabelais' Panurge and then of Gargantua,
sends his penis across a pond, lodging it in the chief's
daughter, until an old crone armed with an awl forces
him to withdraw; he changes into a woman and marries the chief's son; he falls from a tree into a mountain
of his own dung. After various other adventures, Trickster recalls that he has a mission and proceeds to remove obstacles to navigation from the Mississippi and
then to displace a troublesome waterfall from a lake.
Finally he takes his last meal on earth and departs, first
into the ocean and then to heaven.

Although the world of Trickster is only incipiently
human (we cannot tell human beings from birds and
animals, and Trickster addresses every object, quick or
dead, as "little brother"), his human purpose gradually

emerges as the cycle continues. His self-transformation into a woman softens his irresponsible laughter at himself and at the sufferings of others and sends him back to his family. This is the first step toward what Radin calls "socialization," and it indicates the cultural purpose of the whole cycle. This purpose is to depict man in his culture—culture in general but also a particular culture with its own traits, prestige values, institutional instabilities and ideological contradictions.

The stories of Hare, Red Horn, and the Twins are concerned with the correction of Trickster's chaotic world and have for their theme a basic tenet of Winnebago culture: that the lowly individual can rise to high estate by means of the creative energy of his inner self provided that this energy is directed toward the cultural goals of the tribe. The first task of these stories is to define man as a social animal and to give him his just measure of independence from the gods and from the natural world. The second task, already operative as early as the Hare cycle, is to establish a concept of *hybris*, to dramatize the fact that there are limits of aggrandizement and irresponsible freedom beyond which no man may go unpunished. The Winnebagos, you see, have their idea of tragedy. At the end of the Twins cycle, the Twins in their infatuation have slain one of the animals who serve as pillars upholding the earth. And from their crime they turn submissively to the god Earthmaker, saying that "something terrible is chasing us." The Twins pass beyond the upper limits of culture, whereas Trickster exists below the lower limits. The fundamental motive and meaning of these stories would seem to be the necessity men feel to delineate artistically the boundaries of conduct as their culture understands them, to dramatize the forbidden joys and consequent suffering of those who transgress the boundaries, and so to trace the path of the individual in relation to the community from birth to death.

MAGGIE: A most moral mythology.

RALPH: More so than most, it seems to me.

MAGGIE: Had Mr. Blowsnake any dying gods?

GEORGE: Dying gods? No, not one. But how do you like my story?

DOROTHY: I think Trickster is very true to life. He reminds me of Bobby at age three or four. But Mr. Blowsnake should have made him afraid at some point. Little boys who are full of turbulent fantasies of aggression and destruction very readily project that large burden of turmoil onto the universe. Hence, they are the ones who come to mother trembling and weeping during a thunderstorm, when Earthmaker roars in the sky. The storm seems to them to be the consequence of their bravado; they are afraid because they thought they were the sole proprietors of all that disorganized discharge of instinctual drives, and now they have been made to feel fearfully small for such big dreams. What they need at this point is reassurance and a humane and ordered authority which should gradually take the place in their minds of the sheer potency of instinctual fantasies. It is an important step toward mastery of the external world.

NANCY: I think George's story proves that many of the things Ralph criticizes my generation for are necessary attributes of culture as such. Apparently, "other-directedness" is not an invention of modern suburbanites. If the Winnebagos discovered in the wilds of Wisconsin, or wherever, that life must be conducted by rules, danger signals from the group, prestige values, and so on, who am I to deny the human need for such things? Hare and Red Horn are not too clear to me, but they seem to be the well-acculturated people who are ready to learn from the mistakes of unstable characters like Trickster and the Twins.

RALPH: Obviously no civilization will be bearable without certain taboos, rules, and unspoken assumptions about the limits of conduct. But whereas Nancy seems disposed to justify Trickster and the Twins only as horrible examples for the edification of Hare and Red Horn, I would rather put it that no civilization is tolerable without plenty of people in it who respond to the spirit of play and uninhibited fantasy represented by Trickster and who do not shrink, for prudential reasons, from the god-defying aspiration of the Twins. That society is unfortunate which is bent on dwindling down the promethean impulses into community decorum.

DOROTHY: Despite his obvious interest in interpersonal relations, Mr. Blowsnake seems to have had a solid Freudian education. At least I notice that he alludes to the oral, anal, and phallic stages of development. He appears to insist on the central significance of sex.

NANCY: Yes, but don't you think that sex itself changes from generation to generation because of different cultural assumptions.

MAGGIE: It seems to go on and on and——

RALPH: Sex becomes suffused with different emotions, fears, and ideals in different decades. For instance, the advanced spirits of the Depression period tended to confuse sex and ideology. I suggest as an extreme example of this the sexual intercourse that took place in proletarian novels at the moment when violence broke out at the struck plant. There was a desire to incorporate into the personal life the fated working out of revolution and history. The orgasm was a symbolic revolution, a loss of self like the immersion of oneself in the proletarian cause, or possibly, for many guilt-ridden middle-class rebels, a symbolic suicide.

NANCY: How did sex take place in the 1920's?

MAGGIE: Are you asking me, darling? If the literature of the period is any guide—Fitzgerald, Sinclair Lewis, even Hemingway—it didn't so much take place as just get dreamed about and talked about.

DOROTHY: And in the 1950's it takes place all about us, in the open as it were. The typical modern commuter's physiognomy bespeaks a steady satisfaction with the marriage bed. His wife, whose mother could remember achieving a complete satisfaction during intercourse only twice in her twenty years of sexual activity, has hopes of being fulfilled on an average of twice a week for forty years.

RALPH: Well, I have no doubt that the steadily rumpled suburban bed, as George likes to call it, is a good thing for everybody's health and nerves. Still, don't you feel something is lost when sex becomes, as it were, a group activity, when it becomes an integrated part of the organizational life. David Riesman has spoken of sex as "the last frontier." This appears to make sex a beckoning unknown territory, the undiscovered country. And it implies, to me at least, that sexual intercourse is not only a close communion of the partners but also a personal, even a private and lonely, adventure.

NANCY: I think that is an old-fashioned idea. Certainly the lonely orgasm of the olden days produced anxiety.

RALPH: Are you sure that loneliness in this respect is a thing of the past? What I mean is——

DOROTHY: Love-making for the older generations was more subject than it is now to all the strains and hidden hysterias of the incompletely resolved Oedipus complex. Also the partners felt the guilt and tensions

of their moral, religious, or political commitments—
there was always a third Presence at the marriage bed,
one's Father or Mother or one's God or one's Ideology.
People nowadays have succeeded in dispelling some
of the terrible old ghosts, I should imagine.

RALPH: But in doing so they have also dispelled
some of the mystery. They have freed sex of an old
melodrama and substituted a comedy of bourgeois
sentiment or a soap opera.

DOROTHY: Being a student of the soap opera I can
report that although the Oedipal melodrama has been
somewhat dispelled, all is not well in the suburbs. Despite the frank and solid satisfactions of modern sex—
anxiety, fear, and unhappiness are still to be found in
the bedroom. Failure in love-making is no longer the
result of fearing to violate a private taboo or ideal. It
is the result of the general anxiety that comes of fearing that you can no longer keep up appearances. The
appearance of success, of friendliness and good will, of
topnotch competence in every department of a formal-
ized but nonetheless complex mode of life—all this
exacts from the slave of public opinion a great price,
both moral and physical. In the row on row of meticu-
lously neat houses and clipped lawns, a plot of un-
mowed grass, a dingy shutter, a car four years old pro-
duces an immediate impression of squalor. Inside the
house too, particularly a house of really modern design,
a vase of wilting flowers or a brassière on a chair, pro-
duces a sordid effect, although they would not have
done so in the big old-fashioned three-story frame
house. The old houses were built by people who recognized a certain amount of squalor, unsuccess, and
deviation from the norm as a part of life itself. These
houses admitted to the world their understanding that
appearances may be misleading. The new houses, and
the people in them, are committed to denying this so

obvious human truth. And the result is that although old anxieties have been banished, new ones have been created.

RALPH: I imagine the old ones are still around. The Oedipus complex is human fate and not just an oddity of the late nineteenth-century Viennese bourgeoisie, as the anti-Freudians say. Of course, its manifestations change from culture to culture, but it remains formidable and more or less fixed, at least in any energetic and complicated civilization. Almost anywhere that you scratch away the confident smiling surface of middle-class life, you are likely to find hysteria and anxiety, shock treatments and the excessive use of sedatives and alcohol. Surely, all this cannot come merely from the pressure to be "other-directed"; it must come in large measure from the Oedipus situation—the great source of human strength and human weakness.

NANCY: But don't you feel that Riesman, Fromm, and Sullivan have freed us from the Oedipus complex?

GEORGE: They have certainly shown us much about contemporary American culture that seems to make the Oedipal conflict obsolete as a theory of character. At least it has had to be drastically revised. The stern retributive father and the rebellious, castration-haunted son seem to be archaic types. We now have a more fraternal and relaxed society. On the cap of each bottle of milk we received this summer was printed the word RELAX. The son who suckles at his mother's breast now sees the same word in his mind's eye; he cannot be haunted by uneasy desires of seduction, such as Freud imagined him to feel.

RALPH: But if that is true, won't he grow up without any native capacity for rebellion or as far as that goes, for seduction? Won't he grow up without any ingrained idea of retribution and authority?

GEORGE: To some extent, yes. And so much the better off he will be, during his tender years and later too. He will learn in good time the meaning of rebellion and authority, and he can congratulate himself on living in a society where authority is softened by persuasion and understanding and where rebellion need be no more than mild.

RALPH: Yet it seems to me that Freud's idea of the Oedipal conflict, even if partly mythical, is one of the great cultural images of all time (and, after all, he didn't invent it). I doubt if we can afford to indulge the mild fantasies of escape which urge us to reject it. What else gives such clear and strong definition to human character and human fate? What other symbol gives such significance and resonance to our daily living or fills our waking and sleeping moments with such drama and such power? Are human beings to lose all sense of guilt, bereavement, and rebellion? Will they no longer know the joy of achieved freedom?

GEORGE: Many cultures have decided that the Freudian life of psychic violence is sustained only at too great a cost in human suffering. They have modulated and revised the Oedipal conflict until it hardly exists as such. My notion is that America has finally succeeded in developing such a culture. I look forward to its further evolution with confidence and satisfaction. We shall find less shocking and painful sources of the rewarding psychic life.

RALPH: I have the feeling, again, that George and Nancy are mistaking the present age of prosperity and suburban placidness for eternity. What strikes me as only a materially fortunate interim period in American history strikes them as the mature and settled America finally achieved. We shall see.

DOROTHY: It is getting late and the children must be fed.

MAGGIE: Ralph is a willing summarizer—before you

go, please state what have been the fruits of the afternoon's conversation.

GEORGE AND NANCY: Hear, hear.

RALPH: I will if you will help me. We have been talking about the interim or cold-war state of mind. At its best it has been a time of revision and introspection, of concentration on the particularities and concrete intricacies of life. Anatole Shub says that for the intellectuals—those who are interested in literature, politics, moral questions, and the social sciences—it has been a time of "withdrawal." The tendency of this era has been to study the unit—the single literary text, the individual psyche, the family group, the suburban community. This navel-gazing, this introspection and concentration on the isolated unit has given us a new and valuable sense of the immediate fact—the literary fact, the psychological fact, the family and community fact. Yet the mind has been drawn away from the big picture—from history, from politics, from the ideology of culture. The consequence is that as we have become more subtle and discriminating, as we have gained more expertness in the local and limited areas of human life, our minds have tended too much to mysticism, to an exaltation of the helpless middling emotions, to a pietistic quietism. Withdrawing, not according to plan but for withdrawal's sake, we have grown inert, purblind, and fatalistic.

GEORGE: What would the plan be, if we had withdrawn according to it?

RALPH: Well, of course, it would be the "return" to action in the world, a return that would be the main justification of the withdrawal. A withdrawal justifies itself if, like sleep, it is a period of refreshment and preparation. Yet the strongest impulse of our time is to withdraw in order to escape from the world, or, if the purpose is to be reborn to a new life, it is a life of transcendence and denial. Wouldn't it be inspiring if now the mind could be seen to be stirring into a new life and a new realism, and if there should appear a resurgence of radical awareness and action?

MAGGIE: Yet you yourself speak of the American mind as being mostly free of such spiritual experiences, of deaths and rebirths, and withdrawals and returns.

RALPH: Still, as applied to whole societies, such terms are suggestive metaphors. They help us to understand what everyone would admit—that American civilization, like any other, goes through periods of action and of inaction. Matthew Arnold's less spiritual terms seem broadly applicable to our situation. The period of the last fifteen years has been an "epoch of concentration." If things turn out as one might wish, the next decade may be an "epoch of expansion." In any case, Arnold's great essay, "The Function of Criticism at the Present Time," makes very good reading just now.

GEORGE: It seems to me that Ralph is incorrigibly bent on reviving the past. He wants to go out and do battle with the enemy, as in the twenties the intellectuals fought puritanism and Babbittry and as in the thirties they fought fascism and the reactionary aspects of capitalism. He wants to mount a new ideological offensive. What he fails to realize is that there is no tangible enemy and that furthermore the age of ideology is past. You can't fight a war if there is no field of battle, no weapons, and no enemy. To put it simply, the great world problems that confront us moderns are not susceptible of definition by ideology, dialectic, or large-scale intellectual formulations of any sort.

Ralph has cited Anatole Shub's contribution to the *New Leader* series of articles on the Young Generation. Let me quote Daniel Bell's article. He says that "the ideologist—Communist, existentialist, religious—al-

ways wants to live at some extreme, and criticizes the
ordinary man for failing to live at the level of grandeur.
One can try to live heroically if there is a genuine possibility that the next moment will be, actually, a 'trans-
forming moment' when salvation, or revolution, or
genuine passion can be achieved. But such chiliastic
moments are illusions. And what is left is the unheroic,
day-to-day routines of living." So, it would seem that
there has been no "withdrawal." There has been,
rather, a new realism and a general scaling down of
ideological pretensions to correspond with the lives we
actually lead in America. We have merely been going
about the business of the world. Certainly we have not
been doing it perfectly, but we have been doing it
fairly well, and I persist in regarding American culture
as a success. Because it is, there is no need for a "return" or for an "epoch of expansion," even if such
grandiose ideas can ever be said to have any real content. What is needed is a steady growth of wisdom, a
steady application of the intelligence to the daily problems that confront us, an increasing mastery of the human arts of life.

DOROTHY: With my residual Depression-period capacity for asking the literal and obvious question—what
about the hydrogen bomb?

RALPH: What indeed?

GEORGE: It is too tremendous for the individual
mind to conceive or to hope to control. One must count
on an international, or perhaps a superhuman, balance
of forces to make it impossible to use atomic power
for any but peaceful purposes. The bomb, you have to
admit, is intellectually and emotionally boring. Neither
it nor its consequences can be grasped by the mind,
except as a distant abstraction.

RALPH: There is something to be said for keeping one's nose to the grindstone, which seems to be

George's idea of how to live. Yet what happens if the floor suddenly falls from under the grindstone, or the roof falls in? It seems to me that there is no shortage of enemies around—even the old ones, like Babbittry, capitalist reaction, and totalitarianism can hardly be said to have expired just because they have taken on new faces. I don't agree, either, that the age of ideology is dead. The critical revisionism of the past decade has certainly made moralists and psychologists out of us, and it has taught us to be properly suspicious of ideology. But why should we think of ideology as coming in "ages"? It is one of the natural and perennial weapons of the mind and is generated anew whenever the mind applies itself, not just to "the art of living," but to social realities as they are working themselves out in history. I doubt if either social reality or history has disappeared, even though the inclination of men to conceive of the two in relation *has* temporarily declined.

And so I claim to be dimly imagining the future, rather than trying to relive the past. Shall we not hope, at any rate, that the great experience of alert minds in the next decade will be that shock and exhilaration which will follow from our suddenly asking the question, What has happened on the great stage of history while we have been playing our closet dramas? What winds have blown up across the meadow while we have been studying our spear of grass? While we have been glorying in our skill at human relations and social mobility, what satellites have invaded our skies? Can our social skills and our cultural mildness control the harsh mutations of history? Can literature survive in the minds of men if it is not understood in its political significance? Is psychoanalysis valuable if instead of freeing imprisoned energies for social reconstruction it merely saddles us with the terrible duty of

self-inquisition? Of what value is the new competence
in family life if, while we have achieved it, we have
surrendered control of the material development of
the country? It is time to ask ourselves if a fruitful and
humane life will be possible at all in an America full
of the flashy and insolent wealth of a permanent war
economy, brutalized slums, rampant and dehumaniz-
ing Levittowns, race hatred, cynical exploitation and
waste of natural resources, government by pressure
group, by executive abdication and by Congressional
expediency, vulgarization and perhaps the destruction
of the schools, not to mention the sporadic flash and
fall-out of "nuclear devices." Here are enemies enough.
Here is the seedbed of new ideologies.

Saturday Night:
Comedians All

It is eight o'clock. Ralph Headstrong and George Middleby are sitting with Maggie on the Motives' wide easterly veranda, which she insists on calling a "deck." Ralph and George have been summoned by Maggie to meet an old friend, Rinaldo Schultz, who has called unexpectedly to announce that he is staying in Annisquam. Rinaldo was born and brought up in Europe and lived in Argentina briefly, but is now an American citizen. When he first arrived in this country, in 1950, and was much in need of help and orientation in a strange world, Maggie had made him her protégé. Although determined from the beginning to be an engineer, Rinaldo attended Ralph's lectures on literature at the University and also got acquainted with George when both were undergraduates. Pleading fatigue and declaring to their husbands that in any case Maggie arouses unworthy aggressive impulses in them, Nancy and Dorothy have declined Maggie's invitation to be present. Furthermore, Darlene's plastic teeth have made her gums sore and consequently she is sulky and needs a night off. As they wait for their friend, Ralph, George, and Maggie gaze out over an agitated sea, which like the sky is dark, except for the rather vicious-looking whitecaps. A thunderstorm is blowing out of the south over the irritable Atlantic. George seems only mildly interested in the drama of sea and sky, but Maggie has become, for the moment, mystically enraptured.

MAGGIE (*stagily*): The sea is beautiful. My dark-eyed mother is stirring tonight. She calls me with her white arms.

GEORGE: I suspected you of a religious streak, underneath all your debunking tendencies. Do you belong to a cult?

MAGGIE: I am a Dionysian.

GEORGE: Are you the bride of the dark god?

MAGGIE: I am the bride and the daughter of Dionysus. In America my beautiful father was discovered for the first time by my generation (or the one just before). We discovered him through intuition and experiment, but Nietzsche explained him to us in *The Birth of Tragedy*.

GEORGE: Wasn't he the bloke that in Greek times you ladies used to kill annually by dismemberment, with wild ecstatic shrieks in the forest glade? What did you have against him?

MAGGIE: Well, he was uppity. You have to take that sort down a peg every once in a while. It was for his own good, the annual dismemberment, and for ours. Every spring my father-lover is reborn, as good as new. Alas, I cannot say the same of myself.

RALPH: But, Maggie, you are beautiful too.

GEORGE: Oh, yes—beautiful.

MAGGIE: The great dark coming up out of the east frightens me, and the wind sweeping through the trees stirs a correspondent motion within. That is why I like the name Maggie Motive. I married Albert mostly for the name, to be frank.

GEORGE: Don't be Frank. Be Maggie.

MAGGIE: Ha, ha.

GEORGE: Thank you for laughing, but it wasn't as good as all that.

MAGGIE (*laughing hysterically*): Ha, ha. Forgive

me. I am not laughing at you or your meager joke. I am laughing at Walt Whitman.

GEORGE: Good. But what's funny about him?

MAGGIE: The lovely wit, alternately grave, ironic, and whimsical, that he interposes between us and his backdrop of dark mysticism, his feeling for death and the sea.

GEORGE: You are a student of Whitman?

MAGGIE: Oh, yes. I got him up when everyone else was solemnly reviving Henry James. He was my project that year (1952)—project number 738, I believe. Number 737 was chair-caning and basket-weaving. I have them all written down in my project book. (*Looking to sea and murmuring abstractedly.*) One must always have a project.

GEORGE: And what is your project now?

MAGGIE: To talk to you, about Whitman.

The sound of tires is heard on the gravel driveway at the other side of the house. Rinaldo Schultz ducks out of his 1951 Chevrolet and into the patio just ahead of the rain. At the front door Rinaldo receives from Maggie a kiss heavily freighted with manners and morals. He delivers to Ralph and George his characteristic handshake—one frank, vigorous pump. Having declined the proffered drink, Rinaldo sits with the others in the living room. As one watches him gazing with obvious pleasure at the modern furniture and the oversized fireplace, one sees a medium-short man of twenty-seven, brisk, alert, and given to much emphatic gesturing of the finely shaped head with the shock of black hair.

MAGGIE: I insist that we talk about Whitman. Rinaldo won't mind. I happen to know that he is fond of Whitman.

RINALDO: Certainly I won't mind. I notice, however, that whenever I talk to the pessimistic and world-weary Americans about Whitman, they think I am a mad European full of naïve optimism and an unexamined belief in progress. They say I have not considered the nature of evil.

GEORGE: But Maggie, you cannot be, as it were, serious in saying that Whitman is funny, I mean as a comic poet is funny. I think of him as uttering vague, humorless, rhetorical assertions about Democracy. Then, too, he keeps solemnly assuring us that he has experienced life to the full, but he never gives us any sense of real experience or knowledge of the actual world. Instead he gives us either empty abstractions or lists of things out of the newspaper morgue, the primer of American history, the dictionary, and the atlas. Of course, he is very "American," but I don't really accept him as spokesman of his country, although I know that many people regard him as such.

MAGGIE: What do you say to that, Rinaldo?

RINALDO: As for Whitman being a comic poet, I believe that he is, although this is certainly not what I would say first about him. First of all he is the celebrant of American material and spiritual progress, of the dynamic, open, productive New World, with all of its brash power. I know that most Americans are ashamed of this side of Whitman, thinking that he is little better than the inspired George Babbitt when he made his passionate speech about the Standardized American to the Boosters Club. But Whitman is not Babbitt, and there is no reason to be ashamed of him, naïve and strident as he occasionally is. It is true that Whitman is very abstract on the one hand and given to making "catalogues" on the other, but I think he makes real aesthetic capital out of this habit of mind. As for being the spokesman of his country, I positively assert that he is—and by no means only as the inspired Rotarian or political prophet but because he reflects many dilemmas and contradictions, many subtle turns of mind and speech that strike me as very American indeed.

MAGGIE: I think George takes him too hard. What is your naïve and unreflecting response to Walt when he says, "I have never read Mill. What did he stand for, teach, saliently promulge?" I wouldn't trade that delicious "saliently promulge" for all the language of *The Golden Bowl*.

GEORGE: It is a delightful oddity, I admit.

MAGGIE: As another test case, what about these lines from "Song of the Exposition" in which Whitman welcomes the muse of poetry as "the illustrious emigre" who has left the fabled haunts of Europe and come to America. She is

Bluff'd not a bit by drain-pipe, gasometers, artificial fertilizers,
Smiling and pleas'd with palpable intent to stay,
She's here, install'd among the kitchen ware!

GEORGE: What do I think of that? Well, that it's a free country and that if Whitman wants to depict the Muse as one of the TV kitchen goddesses of the hard sell, it's all right with me. The lines are amusing. But I should think that you, glamorous amateur, would be the first to object to the rather obvious and deplorable philistinism of taking the erstwhile nymph of the Fountain of Arethuse and plunking her down among the Norges, Hotpoints, and Coldspots.

RINALDO: I think those lines are delightful and witty. I trust my response and leave it to George to worry about philistinism.

MAGGIE: Gaiety and the excellent arrangement of words transmute all, even philistinism. How about the

moment in "Song of Myself" when Whitman pauses before embarking on an evolutionary extravaganza and
gravely observes: "I find I incorporate gneiss"?

GEORGE: Yes, I remember that. It really is a great
comic moment. But the question that bothers me is:
When we smile at something Whitman says, are we
smiling with him or at him?

MAGGIE: I would stake my soul on its being *with* him
in this case, as in most of the Whitman passages I remember best. True, we often laugh at him when he is
not laughing at himself—that has unhappily become
the standard response to Whitman, though it was not
so in my youth. Many of his sillier passages warrant this
kind of laughter. Yet at other times, when Whitman is
functioning as the great comic poet he is, we laugh *with*
him. Sometimes, to be sure, when we laugh with him,
we suspect he is not laughing enough—that his comedy
is more or less unintentional. But isn't it true that in
every great man who has a streak of humor, the humor
is partly unconscious?

RINALDO: That is surely true. I can say, too, that
Maggie has perfectly expressed the response I have
had to Whitman, ever since I had enough English
to read him. A good deal of the true quality comes
through in German, French, and Italian translation.

GEORGE: Did Whitman ever say he was a comic
poet?

RALPH: In effect he did, yes. When one of the Cam-
den friends of his old age called him an incorrigible
"comedian" because of something he had said, Whitman replied that "one might end up worse" and declared: "I pride myself on being a real humorist underneath everything else."

MAGGIE: I don't say that Whitman is first and fore-
most a comic writer. But especially in "Song of Myself" the comic poet is heard—the Dionysian humor of

the poet whose room was adorned, as I remember reading, by two pictures, "one of Silenus and one of Bacchus." But aside from any and all argument, Whitman is funny, he makes me laugh, he makes me smile even oftener. So I simply conclude that this reaction is the proper one and that one highroad to an appreciation of Whitman is his humor. Am I right, Ralph? What do you think of Walt?

RALPH: May I turn that question over to Rinaldo?

RINALDO: I think Whitman is not the greatest of your nineteenth-century writers, but that he is the most delightful and valuable. He is an ever-flowing source of inspiration. From what I know of the critics of the last two decades, they have assumed that because in some obvious ways the Whitman influence has been bad, it has been all bad. They have assumed that whatever was good about Whitman has long since been discovered and its influence exhausted. I am bold enough to assert that they were wrong on both counts. We have already, at least for this epoch, assimilated Hawthorne and most of Melville. We have absorbed from them, that is, whatever can do us any good. Whitman is of the future.

RALPH: I agree with that, although in subscribing to what Rinaldo has said, I would not mean to reinstate Whitman as the "focal center" of American culture—the position assigned to him by Van Wyck Brooks and by the 1920's in general. Whitman's occupation of the focal center is too strongly contested by writers very unlike him, notably Melville. Which is one way of saying that our culture is multiform, and has no focal center.

Maggie is playing the sibyl tonight. But her idea that Whitman is a comic poet does not sound sibylline to me. It sounds both obvious and profound. The comic sense, as the theoreticians tell us, is often born of incongruities and contradictions. Any moderately well-disposed reader of Whitman will see that he is very far from stamping out distinctions and inner tensions with his flow of universals and abstractions and his sometimes neurotic desire to "merge" with everyone and everything. Take another test case:

> Do I contradict myself?
> Very well then I contradict myself,
> (I am large, I contain multitudes.)

The tendency used to be to pass this off as mere bravado, or to use it as proof of the self-confessed intellectual and literary incompetence of the poet, or (if one felt favorably toward Whitman) to say that it referred to a Hegelian universe. If one wanted to defend Whitman, in other words, one felt that it was necessary to justify the contradictions of his personality and of his work or to show that he wrote good poetry in spite of them. But nowadays one should be ready to accept his contradictions as integral oppositions and polarities, not of the Hegelian order, but as the elements of a more or less sustained ironic view with which Whitman regarded himself and the world. There is an intermittent but strong comic intent, which not only appears in poems like "Song of Myself" but is carried over into the great elegiac poems—for example "As I Ebb'd with the Ocean of Life," where the poet momentarily faces the ultimate irrationality of the universe while

> the real Me stands yet
> untouch'd, untold, altogether unreach'd,
> Withdrawn far, mocking me with mock-congratu-
> latory signs and bows,
> With peals of distant ironical laughter at every
> word I have written,

Pointing in silence to these songs, and then to the
sand beneath.

To take Whitman as existing in or through his polarities is the first step toward a fuller acceptance and
enjoyment of his work. It is the poet who "knitted the
old knot of contrariety" that appeals to the reader who
is free of the tiresome old prejudices against our greatest poet.

RINALDO: Most of the professors seem to regard
Whitman as some sort of philosopher, don't they? They
want to "place" him in relation to Neoplatonism, pan-
psychism, and God knows what all. No?

RALPH: Yes. The routine academician likes Whitman the "sublime" poet of time and space, Whitman
the mystic, the stoic, the Quaker, the cosmic thinker.
He pays little attention to Whitman the poet of the
self, and is embarrassed by the poet's boastfulness and
vaunting Americanism. He explains away or discounts
Whitman's poses. He understands Whitman's contradictions, ambiguities, and ironies, not as native to
the man, but as inadvertent results of his intellectual
naïveté.

Thus when Whitman's official biographer remarks
that "this was the real Walt Whitman, undiscriminat-
ing, easily stimulated by noise, color, and movement,
happy to lose himself in the ceaseless flux of people
going and coming," I want to reply: No, that is the mistake of D. H. Lawrence and Santayana and all those
who see in Whitman only his "merging" with experience and do not see the recalcitrance with which Whitman could also meet life. The routine academician
does not understand the Whitman who described himself as "furtive" and "artful." He does not perceive the
alien, neurotic, divided, covertly musing Whitman,
the envious, fearful, power-seeking, sagacious Whit-

man who could stand aside from life and adopt a series
of attitudes toward it.

For after all, however much Whitman might pose as
a burly proletarian with flowing beard, open collar, and
pants tucked in boots, he was in fact a petty-bourgeois
intellectual. His life is a series of such paradoxes and
symbolic gestures. His charlatanism is a part of the
whole man and a part of his work. And, charlatan or
not, one of the most consistently remarkable things
about him is his ability to make out of his life a series
of indestructible ideals, of exemplary acts which belong to any American's cultural heritage. Whitman is
only somewhat less recalcitrant to the miscellaneous
circumstance of his life as the enfeebled sage of Cam-
den, in his late years, than he had been as the nursing
father and hospital visitor of the middle years, or as
the proletarian Pan and Christlike carpenter and common man of the period just before the publication of
Leaves of Grass.

Well, fair Sibyl, what have you to say to all this?
Have you a reprise or a summary?

MAGGIE: It appears that Whitman appeals to anyone who reads him with any fresh excitement as the
comic poet, the elegist, the singer of the plight and
career of the self, the creator both in his personal life
and in his poems of various ideal images which we can
regard with affection and respect.

GEORGE: But isn't there a danger of being too sophisticated about Whitman?

RALPH: Yes. One can even over-respond to Whitman's own sophistication (he is always setting traps
like that), and thus neglect his simplicity, his plain
democratic faith, his undistorted intuition of the natural sources of being. However many ironies and ambiguities his recalcitrance to life may generate, one of
the ways in which he appeals to us is not in the ten-

sions of his mind but in his "loafing," his flowing, pleasurable intimacy with the world around him. It is easy to smile (but wasn't Walt smiling too?) at the surprised and delighted poet who calls himself a "caresser of life," the musing Dionysus to whom life cries "Ahoy! from the rocks of the river." But it is not so easy, so hectic in us are the distortions of will and intellect, to honor Whitman's receptivity to experience and to recognize the liberating effect it had on a hitherto squeamish American mentality.

GEORGE: I see I must have another look at the Good Gray. Still, I don't suppose you deny there is a lot of awful fustian in him.

MAGGIE: Oh, an immense amount.

RALPH: It was there from the beginning, even in his greatest poem, "Song of Myself." And it got worse as Whitman grew older. Despite his isolation and his relatively small circle of readers, Whitman gradually succumbed to the peculiar pressure a democracy puts on its great writers to become self-publicists, pundits, prophets, theologians, and political oracles.

RINALDO: I have noticed that. Now Faulkner seems in danger of this democratic fate.

GEORGE: Supposing that as I reread Whitman, I should find that you are right about his peculiar excellence, still I should protest that he knew little of the actualities of institutional life, of the life of society.

RINALDO: George is right about that. Walt is too preoccupied with the self as something apart from history and from social and political reality. He thinks of it merely in its ethical, spiritual, and literary relations. In *Democratic Vistas* he simply assumes that history is benign and maternal. One of the things that amazes a European reader is Whitman's belief that America is exempt from all such historical catastrophes as overtook "feudalism"—by feudalism, meaning everything

that happened before 1776. In effect, he assumes that
America is exempt not only from historical tragedy but
from history itself. His sense of things in *Democratic
Vistas* is that history really ended at the inception of
the Republic, and that from then on change would
never be radical but would be merely a matter of gradual unfolding and realization. This view is not only historically unrealistic, as viewed by us unhappy citizens
of the atomic age, but it is oddly conservative too.

GEORGE: Yes, I've noticed that. How do we reconcile this conservatism with the usual view of Whitman
as the prophet of the future and the "promulger" of
those radical changes which were supposed finally to
bring about a truly democratic world?

RALPH: Everything Rinaldo says about Whitman's
lack of historical realism is true. As for the contradiction between his conservatism and his radicalism, there
are many things to be noted, the most obvious being
that this contradiction, as I am sure Rinaldo will agree,
is extremely common among Americans. One way of
getting at it is to notice what Whitman meant by
"prophecy." Do you recall what he says in *Specimen
Days*? He says "the word prophecy is much misused;
it seems narrow'd to prediction merely. That is not the
main sense of the Hebrew word translated 'prophet';
it means one whose mind bubbles up and pours forth
as a fountain, from inner divine spontaneities reveal-
ing God. Prediction is a very minor part of prophecy."
Although he is perhaps not speaking directly of social
prophecy, what he says here accords with that sense
he gives us in *Democratic Vistas* that the purpose of
prophecy is to reveal a perfect dispensation already
given, but now debased, distorted, or imperfectly re-
alized. Like many, perhaps most, prophets, Whitman
employs radically novel emotions, an apparently disruptive philosophical indeterminism, and a new lan-

guage in behalf of conservative ideals. And thus in *Democratic Vistas* he commits himself to an implied conservatism strangely at odds with his declared principles.

GEORGE: But is there any intellectual substance to his conservatism?

RALPH: No. Whitman's conservatism is real enough as a prophetic attitude and as a form of instinctive prudence. He makes apparent declarations of principle in his later years, such as "I am a conservative of conservatives." But these do not constitute a "position." So that after all, his conservative tendencies as they appeal to us in his poems and dithyrambic prose remain memorable impulses merely, and do not, on the level of ideas, affect in any way the buoyant democratic idealism which also makes itself felt in *Democratic Vistas* or the radical utopian vision of "Song of Myself" or "Song of the Open Road."

So you see, George, the contradictoriness of Whitman's politics is typical of all the "old knots of contrariety" which are found in his personality and his work. In Whitman's mind political radicalism, though dominant, is held in a state of ironic tension with political conservatism. In *Specimen Days*, Whitman noticed a similar conflict in Carlyle, although in Carlyle he found that conservatism dominated; and he spoke eloquently of the "two conflicting agonistic elements" that "seem to have contended" in Carlyle's mind. We will always be wrong about Whitman, the man and his works, if we think of him as in any way monolithic or single-mindedly tendentious, or if we think of him as being merely confused. Whitman too was "agonistic." And it is not out of any love of literary intricacy for its own sake, but in recognition of the facts and because one wants to arrive at a steady and untroubled appreciation of his simplicities, that one tries to conceive of Whitman in his contrarieties.

GEORGE: As I recall, it was Santayana who said that Americans do not regard Whitman as the "spokesman of the tendencies of his country," that he appeals only to the "dilettanti" and that only foreigners regard him as a representative American.

MAGGIE: I love that "dilettanti"! It's so—so *Italian*.

RINALDO: Santayana has hit on an unhappy truth. I do not understand why Americans disown their great spokesman.

RALPH: Obviously Whitman has never been read by a large proportion of his countrymen. And in our drab decade, the literary people have not responded to Walt. But Whitman really is an authentic spokesman for the tendencies of his country. In describing Carlyle as "agonistic" Whitman recognized the fact that to exist in one's contrarieties is not an exclusively American fate. Yet Whitman's writings show his perception that although American democracy offers to the world an appearance of unrelieved uniformity, contrariety is in fact more nearly of the essence of life in America than it has ever been in any great civilization. We now begin to see, perhaps for the first time, the extent to which the life and works of Whitman exemplify what this fate may mean to Americans. Maggie, I positively suspect you of not listening.

MAGGIE (*who has drifted to the window and is looking out*): You are positively correct. I grow weary of cultural generalizations. I was listening to the imperious voice of the storm. The wind sweeps along the stone wall, and outside the window, where the tall grass and the rosebushes sway like restless souls, the spirits of my ancestors are astir—the one who married an Indian chief in Montana, the poetess who died of too much sherry in the attic in Marblehead, the maiden who was kidnapped and taken to sea by a Portuguese Gloucester fisherman, the stern judge who ruined himself to further the cause of Daniel Webster, the Yale professor, the murdered diplomat, the wronged wife, the . . . the slippered pantaloon.

GEORGE: Alas, I have no illustrious ancestors. My grandpa came from Liverpool and settled the family in Minneapolis. I hardly know who my own great-grandparents were. There are no ghosts in Minneapolis, and no mystery.

MAGGIE: All the great American writers have seen her—in the forests, in the desert places, at the far corner of the meadow, at the turn of the mountain stream, in the dark pond, at sea. "Death is the mother of beauty."

GEORGE (*solicitously*): May I get you a drink?

MAGGIE: Dear George, I begin to like you immensely. You are so—comfortable. So married, so domestic, so communitarian. I yearn to submit myself, like a tired child, to your tender competence and good will. Just now Rinaldo looks too gallant, energetic, and demanding to suit me. As for Ralph, his absurd ego bores me and makes me nervous. Still, I have to admit that except in moments of blessed passivity, I feel that my fate is allied with his and not with George's or Rinaldo's. My soul, if any, knows only Ralph's. Why is that, Ralph?

RALPH: Because George is lucky enough to be temperate and easygoing and Rinaldo creates his own life, whereas you and I are more fated characters. Ridiculous as it may sound, I have in some degree the power of destiny—I mean the capacity, or the comical misfortune, to act as if I were destined to do what I do. You, my beloved Maggie, are like your generation, the cultural principle of which was libido—a furtive, unfolding, automatic libido. You find yourself powerless to control this uncoiling energy by marshaling it into fixed and concentrated forms, by channeling it steadily in a given direction toward a gradually achieved end. Your great virtue is spontaneity. You have been loved by Dionysus and he has given you intellectual and emotional grace. But you are finally helpless in the face of his eternally emergent energy. It frightens and baffles you when it hums inside you with its imperious exuberance. It unnerves you, and in the process of making you restless and energetic, it exhausts you. You are appalled at its cruel indifference to your individual soul and its particular purposes and desires. It drives you with a demonic power, but it is indifferent to you. Hence, George is right to think you religious. Transfixed and entranced by your own unstable energy, you are perforce a mystic. When you are envious and resentful of me, it is because I do not allow my energies to disperse. I concentrate them toward the long-range task.

MAGGIE: You are right. But what is the cost of this power of destiny, as you grandly call it? An absurd intellectuality. You are a petty power politician of ideas. Nevertheless, it appears that whereas I *like* George, and Rinaldo makes me feel like his mistress, I *love* Ralph.

RALPH: Far be it from me to subject so exhilarating a declaration to cold theorizing. Still, it is plain that you love me because you know that in the long run I stand as helpless and aghast before the Dionysian mystery as you do.

RINALDO: I am speechless.

GEORGE: I am a man of much awareness and considerable thirst. If Maggie will let me, I am going to get another drink. But first, allow me to articulate what is in your minds: "It has never occurred to George to be either a Dionysiac or a politician of ideas or a fanatical intellectual. He has stepped down from the ambitious spiritual dialectics of the 1920's and the 1930's into a more equable temperate zone. He has given up the great life, the old college try. He refuses to live dangerously. He has reneged on History. He is hopelessly bourgeois." But, you wait. Every dog has his day—even the vulgar Airedale. I am busily thinking up *ripostes*. Meanwhile, since you are all such wild personalities and devotees of the vine, I will bring you some more drinks.

MAGGIE (*histrionically*): Dear George, for that speech I love you too. But who am I to be dispensing my love? Am I a Lady Bountiful? True, I have had my brush with immortality. I have known joy, life, adventure. A hedonistic poet once referred to my raven locks in a book of verse written in imitation of Dowson, Eliot, and E. E. Cummings and published by an ephemeral press. And one warm summer night in 1928 a Massachusetts Aristophanes uttered a lewd guffaw in my ear on the veranda of the Rockport Country Club. I was eighteen, I had had my first pink lady. Inside, Red Nichols and his Five Pennies were playing "After You've Gone." The Massachusetts Aristophanes, an excellent poet and translator, is now a waspish critic who teaches in a boys' school. He thinks that everyone born after he was is duller than he.

RALPH: Everyone seems to feel that way nowadays. I am aware that despite your declarations of love, you think me rather dull. Did the people of 1910 think the people of 1920 duller than they? And the people of 1900 those of 1910?

MAGGIE: The people of 1920 think *everyone* duller than themselves. And everyone agrees with them, and everyone is right. Here comes George with the drinks.

RINALDO: If I am to be *echt* American, I suppose I must make another attempt to like bourbon. As for jazz, I learned to like that with no trouble at all, even before I came to this country. I wish I could have been with Maggie to hear Red Nichols. But there is a very good combo at the Shore Tavern in Gloucester. Would you all like to go?

This being received as a good suggestion, the party drives off through the rain in Rinaldo's car. The last bit of consecutive conversation is to the effect that the typical band of the twenties was Dixieland—much improvisation and every man for himself until all came to rest in a perilous unity; that the typical band of the thirties was the big, beautifully integrated swing band —the large cooperative effort being symbolic of that decade; whereas the typical band of the fifties was the chamber group with much emphasis on the cool technique and the personality of the soloist. George says the generalization is dubious, and Rinaldo says that he enjoys all kinds of jazz too much to worry about their cultural significance. At two o'clock Rinaldo and Maggie bring Ralph and George home under a clear, starlit sky, and then, as George puts it, "slip into the night."

Sunday Morning:
Conservative Impulse,
Radical Idea

RALPH: Well, George, did you sleep soundly? My sleep was broken as usual after such occasions as last night by a general anxiety. Old-fashioned moralists would call it remorse and sensibly suggest drinking less and talking more circumspectly.

GEORGE: I slept perfectly, thank you. But I guess you rose early.

RALPH: I took Darlene to mass. The cobwebs are not yet cleared from my head. How about a walk over the ledges? The bright sun and the cool salt air may restore me.

GEORGE: Let's go.

RALPH (*as they walk*): Are you a churchgoing man?

GEORGE: No, although I will probably become one, once we settle down somewhere. Nancy has been taking the children to "Family Sunday" at the Episcopal Church this summer. She is the religious member of the family, since the near drowning of the older child two years ago. I have religious feelings. I can admire what I suppose to be the simple piety of Darlene.

RALPH: I'm not sure, however, that she perfectly distinguishes between the saints and the Mother of God on the one hand, and on the other, the glamorous world of Entertainment Personalities she longs to enter. I believe that for her all these are somehow encompassed in the same Heaven. It is the feeling I get from the Ed Sullivan TV show—he puts on a sort of secular mass. The camera centers momentarily on a priest in the audience.

GEORGE: In a different way the same breakdown of barriers has occurred among the Protestant churches. Membership has boomed in the postwar years and in the process the churches have become even less distinguishable from the rest of society than they were before.

RALPH: Yes, the preacher loses all sense of dignity and of a sacred calling, and tends to become a combination ethical counselor, social worker, psychotherapist, group organizer, and Rotarian booster. The lay proselytizers who try to get you to join their church always tell you that their minister is a "straight-from-the-shoulder" type and that there is no nonsense about *him*, meaning, of course, *no religion*. As for the clergyman himself, he has no time for religion, even if he is so inclined. He is one of the army of the underpaid and overworked on whom a thoughtless and childlike society unloads its personal problems. He is always getting "emergency calls" from members of his flock; they are on the verge of nervous breakdown, not wrestling with the Devil—maybe it's the same thing.

GEORGE: You may be right in thinking, as I take it you do, that like the universities the churches have lost much of their special power by allowing themselves to merge with the rest of society, to become merely cogs in the great social machine. It is hard to remember that there was a time when this world stopped at the door of the church and, inside, one dwelt in the City of God. Those who were oppressed and dismayed by the world, even the criminal, found sanctuary in the church.

RALPH: Wouldn't you think that the churches would be better off if they restricted their membership to those who fervently believe and are skillful in the hereditary ritual and language of the church? Wouldn't

religion have more effect on society if it were undeniably different *from* society? Of course, the Catholics
have thought of all this and over the centuries have
launched various elite minority movements within the
Church. As for the Protestants, I imagine it is all a matter of the anguish of the individual. Don't you suppose
that young ministers go out from the Union Theological
Seminary every year, full of Reinhold Niebuhr's profound and demanding crisis theology, only to be driven
to despair by the stupidity and aimlessness of the suburban flocks?

GEORGE: I suppose so. At the same time, I plan to
find out if in the Episcopal churches there isn't a solid
middle ground between the troubled lives of the pa-
rishioners and the sacred calling of the minister, between this world and the City of God. If I am to live
in a community, I want to help make it work, even if
I have to listen to sermons couched in a language that
would have made St. Paul, John Donne, or Jonathan
Edwards shudder.

RALPH: The language will be indistinguishable from
that of the public relations man for a cement company;
the sermon will have been completed by the harassed
preacher at three o'clock Sunday morning. But, I see
that you are a conservative and that you think of the
church as a necessary part of society.

GEORGE: Up to now I have been a conservative by
default. That is, the radical ideas of previous decades
do not seem relevant to the present situation. "The liberal imagination" has been so thoroughly chastised
that it is hard to find much of a positive credo in it.
The radicalism of the past was too often only a projec-
tion of the neurotic stresses and hidden aggressions of
disaffected members of the middle class. And, frankly,
don't you think that much of the reforming idealism
of middle-class radicals is really a revenge upon the

masses? Most reformers were brought up in homes where at least a minimum of good manners and social responsibility was practiced. When they became liberals or radicals they adopted even higher ideals of responsible behavior. Naturally, they are dismayed by the obvious fact that the American populace, like any other, is unruly, coarse, and brutal. Middle-class liberals don't want to liberate the people but only to improve their manners and keep them in their place.

RALPH: A strenuous indictment, and of course it contains much truth, although the truth does not seem to me to lead to the conclusion that liberalism must be abandoned. That isn't an option—in politics we Americans are liberals or we are nothing. I agree with you, however, that any bourgeois liberal who does not admit that he wishes both to liberate and discipline the people is either a dreamy utopian, a hypocrite, or ignorant of his own motives.

GEORGE: But what do you mean by saying that liberalism is our only option? On the contrary, it seems to me that now is the time to construct a conservatism that will suit American conditions. Not that I want to be thought of as merely a conservative, still less a reactionary. I would rather be a liberal-conservative, and help to create a healthy dialectic of liberal and conservative ideas in this country.

RALPH: Certainly "conservatism" is one of the key words of our decade, one of those words by which historians will identify the intellectual and emotional temper of the time. Other such words are "the middle way," "the moral imagination," "tragedy," "tradition," "religion," and words that suggest a complex reality which renders inadequate an oversimplified liberal rhetoric—words such as "ambiguous," "absurd," and "ironic."

But let me propose the following, and then try to

back it up by one or two examples from American political life and American literature: Under American conditions it is impossible to evolve a relevant theory of conservatism. It is thus impossible, and undesirable, that our political life should consist of a theoretical debate between conservatism and liberalism.

Tell me, what conservative thinkers would you draw on for your new conservatism?

GEORGE: On Edmund Burke, primarily. But we have had American conservatives of intellectual power—Madison and John Adams, Randolph of Roanoke, Calhoun, Daniel Webster. One might also emulate such enlightened Republicans as Elihu Root, Stimson, Wendell Willkie, and Senator Case. There are genuine conservative elements in the patrician liberalism of FDR and Stevenson.

RALPH: Well, Burke is the authority most often appealed to by the new conservatives, and writers like Russell Kirk and Peter Viereck have argued from the precepts of Burke to the practice of American politics and American life. But the fact remains that, as someone has said, "In America, Edmund Burke is Thomas Jefferson." This truth is what I want to impress upon you if I can—namely, that the inherited quality of American cultural life depends on a discontinuity between conservative feeling and liberal ideas. As was true of Jefferson, all our impressive and historically successful ideas are liberal or radical, although some of our most important impulses are conservative. But conservative as these impulses are, they are not translatable into ideas, political or otherwise. They are impulses which tend to remain private and personal; like all conservative impulses they urge moderation of behavior and attachment to habit.

GEORGE: Why, then, should they not be translatable into political ideas?

RALPH: Because neither in their origin nor in their ideal goal are they related to evolving political, social, or religious institutions.

GEORGE: But the relatedness we speak of is demonstrated by Burke.

RALPH: But, my dear fellow, Burke lived in England. The source of the conservative impulse in America, as is shown by our literature, is that nostalgia for the simpler, happier way of life which we Americans have felt from the beginning always to be receding into the oblivion of the past. We value with our conservative instincts that which history has already rendered irrelevant to the formation of our ideas. This discontinuity between emotion and thought is in marked contrast to the more nearly organic cultural life of England, which lent relevance to Burke's appeal from tradition and instinct to idea, to his derivation of conservative ideas from conservative emotions. The ship of the new conservatism in this country sinks on the rock—or rather, among the shoals—of the discontinuities of American life.

Do you remember Lionel Trilling's much discussed statement that in the United States liberalism "is not only the dominant but even the sole intellectual tradition"? Trilling went on to say that although there were plenty of conservative and reactionary impulses around, there were (with isolated exceptions) no conservative or reactionary *ideas* on the scene, there were only impulses expressing themselves in action or in "irritable mental gestures which seek to resemble ideas." This suggests to me a fundamental truth which one may hope to see borne out by the future, as by the past.

GEORGE: I think you are wrong. It suggests to me, as I believe it did to most of its readers, that conservative ideas should now come into their own. I go along with the many people, both liberal and conservative,

who say that we would benefit if there were more intellectually respectable conservative ideas around.

RALPH: I do not think we would, because the real
life of our culture is in the perennially unresolved contradiction between our conservative feelings and our
radical ideas. The life of our emotions, our fantasies,
our literature, our daily manners and morals—this
shared cultural life is not at home on a middle ground
whereon radical and conservative ideas have been dia-
lectically engaged and a compromise achieved. The
vital conflict, the energizing dialectic of American life,
is the opposition of idea to instinct and impulse, and
not the opposition of idea to idea.

GEORGE: I begin to see what you are driving at. But
don't you think that practical statesmanship and a successful and humane politics depend in this country, as
in any other, on a perpetual compromise of ideas? And
don't you think that American politics would be more
rational and social progress facilitated if our political
parties represented competing ideologies, instead of
both of them being liberal-conservative coalitions with
no stake in winning an election beyond the spoils and
the glory?

RALPH: Doubtless something might be gained if a
new alignment should emerge which would place conservatives in one party and liberals in the other. Yet
history has gradually brought about a two-party system
in which, despite certain differences of policy and
tradition, both parties tend to mirror the national mentality as a whole. Both parties draft platforms drawn
from the principles of radical democracy and, except
in periods of acute crisis, conduct themselves in office
largely according to conservative instinct, prejudice,
and habit.

GEORGE: It seems to me that you believe that whatever is, is right.

RALPH: In this case it is right, in the sense that it allows 170,000,000 people to live—so far, at least—under conditions preferable to those in any other part of the world. Are you sure your hankering for an ideological realignment of parties isn't potentially revolutionary? At any rate, I don't believe you have much material to work with. Among present-day Congressmen, for example, there are no conservative ideas worthy of the name. The opponents of segregation appeal to the great ideas of democracy; they speak in the name of the Bill of Rights. But except for a few romantic ideologues, the segregationists do not cite Calhoun. Their argument is a nonideological realism which openly appeals to instinct, prejudice, and habit (as has William Faulkner in his comments on segregation).

Despite the notable shortcomings of our two-party system, it is the right and inevitable one under American conditions.

GEORGE: But wouldn't Congress be more effective if issues were more clear-cut?

RALPH: It would be a more impressive debating society than it is. But the perennial ineffectiveness and inertia of Congress are not the result of the ideological weakness of the conservatives but of the reactionary quality of their conservative impulse, combined with the uncertainty and timidity of the liberals. The vitality of American political life thus depends on a twofold dialectic—the dialectic between conservative impulse and liberal idea and the dialectic among liberal ideas.

GEORGE: And you think that what is true of our political life and of our general culture is also true of our literature?

RALPH: Yes, our literature will be found to express conservative sentiments and radical ideas. The deepest emotions of Walt Whitman—as we were saying last night—are retrospective and nostalgic, although he viv-

idly expressed the radical ideology of our democracy.
This contradiction is also to be discovered in more profound and more dramatic writers like Melville and
Faulkner, who sometimes express liberal democratic
values. Yet the real concern of these writers is with contradiction as such—they are concerned, that is, with
those native conflicts of our culture out of which have
evolved our conservative impulses and our radical
ideas.

GEORGE: But surely Faulkner and Melville, Cooper
and Hawthorne, Henry Adams and Edith Wharton advance conservative ideas. It seems to me that one of
the unmistakable signs of our maturity has been the
recent discovery of a genuine conservative tradition in
our literature, to match the liberal optimists of the
Whitman-Emerson tradition. In the darker, more profound writers there is a saving sense of tragedy, of the
reality of evil, of myth, of the limitation of human
powers—in general a conservative humanism with distinct political and religious implications. There has
been, I suggest, an end to innocence.

RALPH: I agree that these writers are more profound
moralists and have more complex imaginations than
Whitman and Emerson. But not that they constitute
any sort of "genuine conservative tradition." Faulkner
does not propound a conservative position or ideology
of any sort, although many good critics claim that he
does. Nor is Melville a classicist or humanist, as some
conservative critics claim. Hawthorne still looks like
the same sturdy democrat and skeptic in morals and religion that he always was, yet lately several writers
maintain that he is Thomistic or a conservative Christian humanist. Many people nowadays seem to take a
secret satisfaction in having learned from a mass-
circulation magazine that Hemingway, although not,
like Darlene, a Catholic, often slips off to attend mass.

Other people, probably not the same ones, seemed to be moved a few years ago when John Dos Passos came out for Senator Taft for president—Dos Passos, who had once proclaimed militantly from the left: "all right we are two nations." And since I have mentioned Senator Taft, it may be worth going on to say that he was like most American writers in that his conservatism was impulsive and nostalgic. Ideologically he was as different from Edmund Burke as possible; he was what he called himself, an old-fashioned liberal. But his guiding passion, like that of many men of his class and generation, was a longing for an earlier, simpler, more hardy, more nearly Anglo-Saxon America, before the great waves of immigration, before big business and big government. This is a feeling expressed by many of our so-called regionalist writers.

GEORGE: But what about the aristocrats—Edith Wharton, Henry Adams, and Henry James? Don't you find in their attempt to imagine the upper middle class as an aristocracy an important literary source of conservatism?

RALPH: No, only of fantasy—in so far as they are supposed to have articulated an available conservative theory or position. Let's take a look at them. It is not surprising that Edith Wharton has been claimed for conservatism. But Blake Nevius, who has written the best book on Mrs. Wharton, is surely illogical to conclude that she is a traditional Christian humanist. If this novelist has any ultimate intellectual commitment, it is to a pessimistic naturalism not far removed from that of certain novelists considerably less intelligent than herself, such as Dreiser. True, she looks back with nostalgia to the brief ascendancy of her class, the old New York mercantile bourgeoisie which until 1870 was able to maintain a patrician way of life. The patrician way of life described in Mrs. Wharton's novels urges

one not only to envy its wealth and amenity but to feel
a certain piety toward civilization itself—a piety which
the triumphant new plutocracy that overwhelmed Mrs.
Wharton's class knew not at all. But, as she herself
insists, her class was intellectually bankrupt.

GEORGE: It is hard to say without sounding false, but
I think one should have what you just called "piety toward civilization." I admire Burke because he was the
first great writer who articulated the grounds of this
piety for modern times. Isn't there much in Henry
Adams and Henry James that stems from Burke? In
evolving an imagination of conservatism it seems to me
that these writers look back to Burke, who made the
first distinctively modern effort to infuse the bourgeoisie with aristocratic values. I don't have to tell you
that when I say that "aristocratic" values are necessary,
I don't mean social privilege, wealth, or snobbery. I
mean the sense of obligation and amenity, the moral
imagination which humanizes the raw economics of
bourgeois money-grabbing and gives depth to our
American notions of social responsibility and "other-
directedness."

RALPH: I'll buy that. But it strikes me that you are
beginning to shift your ground. The conservatism you
have just been talking about is an emotion, a style, an
obligation, but it is not a theory or a political position.
If Adams and James sometimes remind us of Burke,
the Burke they remind us of is not the realistic political
theorist and historian but the romantic moralist and
elegist of aristocracy.

GEORGE: You may be right. But let me explain what
I had in mind when I compared Adams and James
with Burke. Burke was apparently the first writer to
use the phrase "moral imagination." I can quote you
the passage, from the *Reflections on the Revolution in
France.* He is telling us what the revolutionaries pro-

pose to do: "All the superadded ideas, furnished from the wardrobe of a moral imagination, which the heart owns, and the understanding ratifies, as necessary to cover the defects of our naked, shivering nature, and to raise it to dignity in our own estimation, are to be exploded as a ridiculous, absurd, and antiquated fashion."

Ideas furnished by the moral imagination, as you see, though ratified by the understanding, are suffused with the sentiments of the heart. And the heart is moved not only by humane sympathies but by attachment to habit, tradition, and ancient prejudice. Burke knew well the danger of modern abstractions and ideologies when these are allied with revolutionary politics. This is the basis of his great relevance to modern times. . . .

RALPH: True, but he was not sufficiently aware that the moral imagination can as easily smother and destroy valuable ideas as humanize dangerous abstractions. Obviously there can be no free dialectic of ideas until there is a free dialectic of impulse and intelligence, so that intelligence can function with provisional autonomy. The aim of conservatism is always to close out the possibility of dialectic. But I interrupted you. Go on.

GEORGE: Like most of the great conservatives Burke has at the back of his moral imagination the image of a woman insulted, in this case Marie Antoinette. We can waive the famous undergraduate question of whether this particular woman was worthy of Burke's expostulation. The important thing is his symbolic use of her, making her stand for the humane values of the inherited civilization for which countless brave spirits have labored, suffered, and died. The moral imagination, as Burke uses the term, is the imagination of chivalry, of *noblesse,* the imagination of civilization itself considered as a sacred and costly inheritance. He

conceives of the imagination as a sort of knight who
selflessly dashes to the rescue of the insulted lady and
then enthrones her as the vessel and custodian of culture. It is not Burke's fault if the imagination is
forced to enthrone civilization in a shaky temple
around which swirl the threatening hordes of "sophists,
economists, and calculators"—the hordes, that is, of
liberals, commercialists, scientists, rationalists, reformers, shysters, and presumptuous petty-bourgeois *ar-
rivistes* who have made the modern world.

RALPH: Very poetical—both Burke and your rendi-
tion of him. But Adams?

GEORGE: Henry Adams, as he tells us in his *Education* and *Mont-Saint-Michel and Chartres,* also felt that
civilization was beleaguered. Probably the most affect-
ing passage in his works is his description of the Virgin
at Chartres. He pictures the Virgin as the proliferating
symbol of culture. She has that final superior innocence
and simplicity which all the great conservatives, from
Burke to Yeats and Henry James, regard as being
among the most precious gifts, not of primitive conditions or mere naïveté or youth, but of civilization itself.
You remember how he describes the Virgin Queen
Mother—she is the greatest artist, philosopher, musi-
cian, and theologian; her taste is infallible, her sentence final; yet the church has been built for her "as a
little girl sets up a doll house for her favorite blonde
doll." For Adams, the Virgin is the symbol of the creative, humanizing, civilizing force by which he intends
to countervail the Dynamo, the symbol of the vast in-
human forces which history and modern politics and
modern science have turned loose in the world.

RALPH: And James?

GEORGE: The idealized women in his novels are like
Adams' Virgin in being at once complicated and simple. In *The Ambassadors,* Lambert Strether, who re-

sembles Henry Adams as much as the Howells he is usually identified with, is surprised to find that Mme. de Vionnet has "fineness" and "subtlety" and all the infinite variety of "Cleopatra in the play" but that this is "without detriment to her simplicity." Mme. de Vionnet is made in this novel to symbolize the high point of culture, and in his *Notebook* James says she has led Strether, the educable American, to "revise and imaginatively reconstruct, morally reconsider, so to speak, civilization." Thus, Strether abandons his liberal Unitarian conception of things and becomes, through the moral imagination, a conservative.

Strether's last interview with Mme. de Vionnet, which James says is the climax of the novel, involves the author's most famous symbol of the imagination. For as Strether is walking through the streets of Paris toward the fateful interview, we are reminded, by some of the metaphors employed and by the moral meaning of the scene, of James' "dream of the Louvre," the dream which James recounts in *A Small Boy and Others,* and which his biographers tell us is of cardinal importance in understanding the essential quality of his imagination. It is a dream of chivalric counterattack. The dreamer is disturbed from his sleep by his sense of a nameless and threatening monster trying to get in at the door. He bars the door against the demon and then with "straight aggression" and "dire intention" he turns the tables and pursues the nameless enemy down a corridor, which turns out to be the Galerie d'Apollon in the Louvre. The moral imagination, in the sanctuary of Western art and culture, puts to flight the forces which endanger both it and the traditional civilization out of which it has been evolved. Before you object, as I see you are about to do, I have one more candidate for conservatism—Wallace Stevens. He symbolizes the imagination as a "noble rider" who represents the unifying "violence within," as he calls it in his best-known essay, and who rides forth to oppose the "violence without"—the violence, that is, of the modern moral chaos.

RALPH: I don't object to your presentation of these writers and the relations you draw among them, because that was masterly. But I think you overinterpret the facts; the thoughts and feelings you speak of do not culminate in a theory of conservatism. For example, I wouldn't call Yeats, James, Adams, or Stevens "great conservatives." Rather they are in some moods poets of conservatism; they are most convincing when they are most nostalgic and elegiac. Strether doesn't become a "conservative," as far as I can see. Let me read you a sentence or two of a letter from Bob Adamant (as is often the case, I have several in my pocket). He says (in his comfortable epistolary style), "Methinks every crusty schismatic wants to read more into Strether and his adwentures than was put there by HJ. I see him more or less (I hope) as written, that is, a rather plain, bright, sensitive high-minded fellow with a great deal of response but also a vast timidity and unthinking recoil—immensely accommodating but, finally, on *his* terms (which is why it takes him so long to discover the most elementary facts) and, in sum, really 'ruined' by his attendance at Woolett, before the book starts. People just can't see how James can be both so genial and so grim as he really is." So you see, George, it isn't likely that James had in mind any real conversion of Strether to conservatism, or anything else. To sum up, I would say that although the poetry of conservatism, of which you have been speaking, is very moving and has some claim on us as moral sentiment, its general irrelevance to living political ideas and realities is plain. There is no conservative "position" or philosophy to be found in the writings of James or Adams or Stevens.

Adams, the only one of the three with the sort of intellectual equipment that might have led him to construct a philosophy of conservatism, did not do so. He described himself with cryptic irony as a "conservative Christian anarchist" and derived from the contradictions of American life only a despairing poetry of "forces."

GEORGE: Apparently I can only agree with you, and promise myself a rethinking of the whole matter. Meanwhile, I have one more big gun to bring into position: Faulkner, although I know already, from what we have been saying yesterday and today, that you won't agree with me. However, I shall assume the role of happy dogmatist and state that various and loose as his writing is, Faulkner at his best is a conservative writer and a tragic writer who gives us, as tragedy does, great images of harmony and centrality wherein contradictions such as that between impulse and idea are reconciled. His imagination is most deeply moved by the idea of a traditional, organic Southern culture.

RALPH: Well, and I will say at the outset that Faulkner is not "a conservative." He is not, on the whole, a tragic writer but a melodramatist—that is, one who envisions human life as consisting in starkly irreconcilable contradictions. It seems to me that he is a skeptic and humorist, and that although he is respectful to the myth of an ante-bellum aristocratic Southern culture, he never seriously propounds it as an ideal. True, his novels and tales are an eloquent testimonial to the power of his longing for an earlier, agrarian, unsullied America before the Snopeses—carpetbaggers, petty commercialists—blighted the country. But as an allegedly social or political view, I don't see how this differs materially from the elegiac nostalgia of Cooper, Thoreau, Mark Twain, and Hemingway, among many others.

Absalom! Absalom! is often spoken of as a tragic novel. But I think of it as a melodrama akin to *Moby Dick*. The Ahab of the piece, as you remember, is Thomas Sutpen, who comes to Yoknapatawpha County about 1820. Sutpen is a man of tremendous obsessive vitality and will power, and with his wild crew of African savages he carves out of the wilderness a great mansion and plantation. But finally, because of dissension in his family involving a clash of races, and because of the war, Sutpen's grand design fails. His attempt to found a dynasty is abortive, the whole enterprise is a disaster, and Sutpen is left with his baffled question: "Where did I go wrong?" Our understanding of the novel lies in our answer to this question.

GEORGE: I remember a remarkable essay by Cleanth Brooks on that. Brooks says that Sutpen fails because he is all will, pride, and calculating intellect, and thinks tradition and justice are merely abstract coins, negotiable like any other. His "sensibility is dissociated." He tries to appropriate everything abstractly. He has no sense of the emotional, the human price of things. He has no commitment to history, tradition, family, or community, or to his own passional self, which he exploits as readily as anything else. Sutpen is fatally innocent because he does not perceive the incongruity between the rigid simplicity of his "design" and the complexity of the human and natural world upon which he tries to impose it. Brooks goes on to compare Sutpen with Oedipus and Macbeth.

RALPH: Much of what Brooks says is certainly true. But the trouble with his analysis begins with what you just said about Sutpen trying to impose his design. As I read the novel, it is another example of the American or perhaps Puritan drama of the mind—a study of the isolation which results from obsessively backing a misconceived theory or design and driving it through to the catastrophe.

The proper parallel to draw for Sutpen would therefore be Captain Ahab rather than Oedipus or Macbeth. Neither Oedipus nor Macbeth is a monomaniac. They merely want to be as rationalistic and common-sensical as possible. The design of their lives is not something they try to impose; it is something gradually revealed to them out of their unconscious desires and the tragic circumstances of their lives. As I recall, Brooks also describes Faulkner as "a conservative writer" in his essay on *The Sound and the Fury*. He says many good things in that essay, notably that the word "primitivism" so many people apply to Faulkner's writing is misleading. But I don't follow him when he claims that Faulkner believes in a traditional community of which the family and the woman are the basic constituents. It is true that no writer can give us a full idea of the human condition, let alone a tragic or religious idea of society, unless he can depict convincingly real women of sexual age—as do Shakespeare, Molière, or Henry James. This is not the occasion to discuss Faulkner's women. But the fact is that he has only two or three interesting ones who are not either brittle flappers, effete aristocrats, moon goddesses, or old maids—Dilsey and Mrs. Bundren and Ruby Lamar. Faulkner succumbs as easily to the subcivilized folk demonology of women as do Cooper, Melville, Mark Twain, and Hemingway. Like these writers, Faulkner is the bard of the masculine life. His attitude toward women, like his attitude toward culture, is usually one of suspicion, mockery, caricature, and even vindictiveness.

Why try to remove the vital contradictions of Faulkner's mind? They are the source of his great art. If Faulkner is in some of his impulses a conservative, he is also an anarchist; if he is traditional, he is also a modernist. If there is one Faulkner who admires a traditional aristocratic community guided by received public values, there is another Faulkner who sees no good but in a life on the utmost margins of a society which one has repudiated in order to live by the purely personal virtues of renunciation, the skill of one's calling, humor, and a sort of stoic contemplativeness.

GEORGE: I can agree with much that you say. At the same time I have two objections to your general argument. Both objections refer to what seems to me your tendency to hypostatize your dialectic instead of merely using it as a method of discovery and provisional definition. First, the matter of tragedy versus melodrama. I know that you do not deny tragic significance to some of the writings of Faulkner, Hemingway, Melville, Hawthorne, and the others. But I think that the lure of system-making and polemical simplification leads you to insist too much on the melodramatic quality of American literature. Faulkner, you see, has the great gift, despite his eccentricity and lack of available moral ideas, of being able to conceive his novels as situations, as dramatic conflicts which are resolved, not in anything so abstract as dialectic, but in dramatic action, in the completed circuit of events. I would agree that the form or convention of a book like *Absalom! Absalom!* or *Moby Dick* is melodrama but that, taking them as wholes, these books have tragic significance. I don't mean merely that they "feel" tragic, nor do I mean to give them any sort of ethically honorific status. Rather, it is a question of how much is committed to the dramatic test, how much is staked, how deep a sense of human life and society is put on the block. In *Absalom!* Faulkner makes a kind of composite image of the high virtues and shows them acting self-destructively in high causes, even though no one character embodies enough of them in himself to measure up to Macbeth or Oedipus.

So, I would say that your view of the matter is true and enlightening, but that it does not exclude what I have just said. You would be on firmer ground if you argued that in the American novel, melodrama and tragedy go hand in hand, partly because the American mind has always fed itself on melodrama and only *through* melodrama can it be brought to see the truth. I say all this with due regard to the fact that you know infinitely more about American literature than I and that you feel a far-reaching and instinctive sympathy with it which I cannot share. I think of myself as thoroughly American, and yet I don't feel at ease with many of what are obviously the greatest works of our literature. For example, I do not think that *Moby Dick* reflects the true qualities of our civilization as accurately, or as profoundly, as James' *Bostonians* or Howells' *Modern Instance*. I find much of the most brilliant American literature extreme, abstract, fragmentary, and, well, *odd*. It is not morally involved in day-to-day living. Perhaps I am all wrong about this. But I claim that my distance from the object allows me, in some ways, to see it more clearly than you.

My second objection to your general argument about conservatism is a very simple one. It strikes me that your notion of an "idea" as opposed to an "impulse" or a "sentiment" is somewhat artificial. I don't feel as confident as you do of being able to tell where the impulse stops and the idea begins. In speaking of conservative impulse and radical idea, you sometimes make a too arbitrary assignment of qualities, an assignment dictated by your polemical purpose rather than by your sense of the reality of things.

RALPH: Your objections are well taken, and I shall have to scale down the pretensions of a dubious dialectic. I am aware that you have forced me to claim less finality for my definitions and to regard them more as a critical approach, valuable not in itself but for what it discovers about American culture and for a certain kind of radical emphasis in cultural criticism, which may be of use in a time when there is little radical criticism of any sort.

With these provisos in mind, let me sum up, adding by the way a brief comment on Mr. Eliot and his sensibility. Then I suggest that we return to the house and get the can of cold beer I see in my mind's eye. Well, then, the fundamental purpose of conservatism must always be to remove, to reconcile, or to gloss over contraries and polarities. For such oppositions, whether in institutional and political life or in our minds, are the perennial source of unrest and change. The opposition we have had before us is the one between impulse and idea, which is to say, in American culture: conservative impulse and radical idea. Naturally programmatic conservatism looks to literature for a reconciliation of impulse and idea, since literature could hardly exist without an interpenetration of the one by the other.

But what lesson is to be drawn from this fact? None except an aesthetic one. It does not follow, because literature has its peculiar ways of fusing emotion with thought, that this fusion is an ideal to be achieved everywhere or anywhere in the general life of the mind and of culture. This mistake is made by Eliot and his followers, when they extend his famous phrase, "the dissociation of sensibility," from a criticism of faulty poetry to a general criticism of modern culture. Certain valuable literary effects depend on a fusion of thought and emotion. Others, common in American literature, depend positively on Eliot's bugbear, the dissociated sensibility. And so does a free dialectic of mind and culture.

The interpenetration of impulse and idea is, as I say, native to American literature, as to any other. But in comparing and evaluating different literatures, the question is where, after all, does the essential quality of a literature rest—in the final reconciliation of these contraries or in a sustained tension between them. In much of the most characteristic American writing, impulse and idea are forced far apart into a radical opposition. Often character is defined by the very alienation of intellect and will from emotion—witness the archetypal Captain Ahab. The life of the best American novels and poems depends on an imagination that is contradictory, unstable, disruptive, fragmentary, and extreme—a fact which defines both the marked successes and the peculiar shortcomings of our literature.

In preserving a vivid distinction between conservative impulse and radical idea, American writers—Melville, Hawthorne, and Faulkner no less than Emerson and Whitman—disqualify themselves as conservatives. In the essentials of their art they both mirror and reassert a secular, skeptical, democratic world.

George and Ralph are drinking beer on the porch; the blue sea is distantly visible. Everett, age four, threatens a sore throat and so has not accompanied the others to the pit. He sits on the floor in the sun, leaning against the railing, and moodily sucks a Coca-Cola bottle, having punched a hole through the cap with hammer and nail.

GEORGE: What you were saying before interests me very much. But supposing that I agree with you provisionally that a reasoned or programmatic conservatism is neither possible nor desirable at present—it would still seem to me that any sort of radical position is even less possible. Does your friend Randolph Bourne have anything good to say on this point—I see

his *History of a Literary Radical and Other Essays*
peering out from under the *Times Book Review* on the
coffee table.

RALPH: Excuse me, while I shove the *Book Review*
behind the shutter here. It makes me nervous. It wishes
me to believe every Sunday morning that good literature is "heart-warming," "wise," "stimulating," and
"provocative." The unwelcome assumption is that I am
cold, foolish, and torpid, and should therefore immediately order the recommended books. But seriously,
doesn't it disturb you that the *Book Review* has become a platform from which all the old radicals sneer
with a corrupt complacency at everything that has
been written since 1940—unless, that is, it conforms to
middlebrow attitudes? Don't you resent its cynicism
and aimlessness, and its enormous influence on literary opinion?

GEORGE: No, I can take it or leave it; no use attacking the impregnable.

RALPH: Well, as for Bourne, his writing was rather
thin in its emotional quality, and of course he did not
live long enough to really find a voice. Yet some of
these essays are excellent. To put it very generally the
two traditions within which he wrote were those of
Whitman and of Nietzsche. In this he was in the main
line of modern American "literary radicalism." For except in the thirties, when economic and political pressures brought the Marxist tradition into the picture and
gave new urgency to native reform movements, these
have been the two great liberating influences on American thought during the last sixty years. Have you read
Bourne?

GEORGE: No, I always thought he was negligible, an
oddity on the literary scene.

RALPH: Then I call your attention to a great passage
in the essay to which he gives the Nietzschean title,

"Twilight of Idols." He suggests to me that in his time as in ours, radicalism means responding to the "allure" of the "thorough malcontents" if, that is, any can be found. It means "irritation at things as they are, disgust at the continual frustrations and aridities of American life, deep dissatisfaction with self and with the groups that give themselves forth as hopeful." Let me read a little more from this fine essay. Bourne says, "they are quite through"—the malcontents—"with the professional critics and classicists who have let cultural values die through their own ineptitude. Yet these malcontents have no intention of being cultural vandals, only to slay. They are not barbarians, but seek the vital and sincere everywhere. . . . They will be harsh and often bad-tempered, and they will feel that the break-up of things is no time for mellowness. They will have a taste for spiritual adventure, and for sinister imaginative excursions. It will not be Puritanism so much as complacency that they will fight. A tang, a bitterness, an intellectual fiber, a verve, they will look for in literature. . . . They are . . . entangled emotionally in the possibilities of American life. . . . They will give offense to their elders who cannot see what all the concern is about, and they will hurt the more middle-aged sense of adventure upon which the better-integrated minds of the younger generation will have compromised. Optimism is often compensatory, and the optimistic mood in American thought may mean that American life is too terrible to face. A more skeptical, malicious, desperate, ironical mood may actually be the sign of more vivid and more stirring life fermenting in America today. It may be a sign of hope. That thirst for more of the intellectual 'war and laughter' that we find Nietzsche calling us to may bring us satisfactions that optimism-haunted philosophies could never bring.

Malcontentedness may be the beginning of promise."
Does this sort of thing appeal to you, George?

GEORGE: Yes, but only as a sort of fantasy out of the
past—it is all so much against the grain of the time. I
suspect that behind Bourne's words there is personal
bitterness, not to say neurosis.

RALPH: Undoubtedly, but does that necessarily affect their truth or falsity?

EVERETT (*musing quietly to himself*): Am I God?
Am I God?

RALPH: What say?

EVERETT: Mama says God is everywhere.

RALPH: Yes, He is everywhere.

EVERETT: Then if God is everywhere, He must be
in me, and I am God.

RALPH: Yes, that's true—don't you think you should
either finish up the Coke or put it in the refrigerator?

EVERETT: OK.

RALPH: Well, then, radicalism today is basically
what it was when it was launched by Bourne, Van
Wyck Brooks and their associates in the years between
1912 and 1918. We are more fortunate than Brooks and
Bourne, because *they* are a part of our radical tradition.

GEORGE: Is this radicalism political?

RALPH: I go along with those who say that politics
is the best possible secular base of culture. So that
fundamentally the radicalism I am talking about is political. But at present, in its immediate applications,
radicalism is not political or economic.

In the long run any sort of cultural radicalism that is
isolated from politics will grow bloodless and irrelevant to the perennial human questions. But the point
is that radicalism is a method, a polemical attitude, an
attack. It does not pretend to be timeless truth. Therefore it must be acutely aware of what it can and cannot
do at a given moment in history. For the moment,

American politics and economics, on the domestic scene, appear impenetrable, mysterious, and roughly successful. A revolutionary politics or economics makes no sense as applied to contemporary America. What does make sense, in improving our economic and political life, is the liberal virtues: moderation, compromise, countervailing forces, the vital center, the mixed economy—although it is high time these were implemented instead of merely being used as rhetorical window dressing.

But the virtues just referred to are those we do *not* want to invoke in our criticism of the general culture—that large complex of sciences, arts, and letters, aesthetic attitudes, manners and morals, public poses and gestures, opinions, tastes, shared fantasies, humor, slang, folk tradition—in short, the vital medium in which we live when we are doing something more than merely existing. The general culture has recently been showing anew its nearly fatal tendency, whenever we let its energy and vitality flag, to collapse into middlebrowism, compromise, centrality, the middle way. At the present time, these are not virtues in American culture; they are its bane.

GEORGE: I don't see how you can force such a gap between what is, or should be, organic—between politics and culture. Isn't this just an academic stratagem to get yourself off the hook—to allow you, that is, to be radical in merely literary and cultural matters without mingling in the dangerous realities of politics?

RALPH: The forcer of the gap, such as it is, is not I but history. In American civilization there is a less continuous line of influence between the intellectuals and political government than in European countries. But the gap is not unbridgeable, and at times, as in the 1930's, the intellectuals take a direct hand, or, to put it another way, culture bears directly upon politics.

Thus, if one helps to create a radical culture which brings about beneficial political change either directly or in the long run, there is no illusion about one's achievement. There is no doubt that the Enlightenment culture of the *philosophes* helped to bring about the French Revolution, and the recent Hungarian revolution stemmed in considerable part from the intellectuals, poets and artists, as well as the workers—and be it noted that the intellectuals involved were exactly those supposed by most people to be out of touch with reality—the despised highbrows of the avant-garde.

But as for our American situation, it is a matter of tempo and the deployment of forces in accordance with what the historical situation demands. In the 1930's the advance shock troops of the radical movement were political, because it was specifically the political function that was in desperate need of reform. The general culture, in contrast to that of our day, was by no means in bad shape. Now the situation is reversed. The very success of the political and economic system, illusory as this may eventually prove to be, has been won at the cost of a general desolation of culture. We have become rich at the cost of forgetting how to live, for where you see among ordinary Americans a new aesthetic expertness and a new interest in the art of living, I see merely a nervous desire to consume anything and everything that can be consumed, a shallow and dreary epicureanism. For these reasons, the first task of radicalism nowadays is directly cultural and only indirectly political and economic. If this be contradictory, let us consider it to be one of the invigorating contradictions we live with, in a civilization that defines itself, on the rare occasions when it has the courage to do so, by its contradictions. Randolph Bourne might have seen the necessity for making the distinction between culture and politics clear had he lived longer. Van Wyck Brooks seemed on the verge of seeing it, but his interests went off in other directions and he became more and more in all things the middlebrow. It has been said that Brooks "abdicated" his position of cultural leadership after his early works. If so, it was not only because he was tired and took the easy way but because his impossible dream of an organic liberal nationalistic American civilization led him to apply the precepts which are suitable to a liberal politics and economics to culture and literature as well. It was thus that he failed us, after his brilliant beginning.

GEORGE: So you base your idea of radicalism on what you were saying yesterday about America being a culture of contradictions?

RALPH: Yes. Both our thinkers and our imaginative writers have been at their best and, it is possible to wager, at their most characteristic when they were mindful of contradictions. As I was saying yesterday, the best critics of American culture have always remarked on the split between spirit and instinct, intelligence and action, art and reality, theory and practice, the highbrow and the lowbrow. Most of these critics have recommended, in all departments of our civilization, a healing attitude of mediation, reconciliation, and middle-of-the-wayism.

It has never been possible until our time to say with conviction that such an attitude is healing in some areas of our civilization but damaging in others. To be radical now is to be able to respond to the "skeptical, malicious, desperate, ironical mood" that prepares one to affirm the cultural virtues of this very cleavage that haunts the moralists and distresses the middle-of-the-roaders. After all, irony, wit, dialectic, drama, finally intelligence itself—all are impossible without a sharp sense of contraries and oppositions. Why should a culture of contradictions not glory in being what it is? As Whitman gloried in America and in himself because both were contradictory.

EVERETT (*who has red hair*): Are you different if you have red hair?

RALPH: Ask George.

GEORGE: Oh, yes, I imagine it makes you different. But in a good way; people like redheads. At least, I do.

EVERETT: I don't like other people who have red hair. (*Sips Coke.*)

RALPH: Ev, how about feeding the goldfish? There is still some Quaker Oats in the pantry.

EVERETT: OK. Then I will go to the dogs.

RALPH: Tell Mrs. McClellan her dogs have run off with two of our shoes and one diving mask.

EVERETT: OK.

GEORGE: I can see that Everett is a born dissenter. The world will never make an organization man out of him.

But supposing, for the sake of argument, that radicalism is possible in the Eisenhower Age, where is it? I mean, there is no one to articulate it. Where is the avant-garde?

RALPH: In its critical function it is wherever anyone is trying to give a true account of the history and nature of our civilization. But let us look at this matter in more detail. Like most people nowadays, you think the avant-garde is dead. I can only reply that under modern conditions the avant-garde is a permanent movement.

GEORGE: I take the cultural vanguard seriously. I am not one of those who reach for a pistol when they hear the word "avant-garde." I am aware that at certain periods in the past the avant-garde of writers and artists has been a necessary part of the cultural economy, and that the general health of culture has benefited by its impulse to experimentation, its search for radical values, its historical awareness, its flexibility and receptivity to experience, even its polemical intransigence. But I am not temperamentally drawn to that sort of thing. And as for today, it seems to me that anyone who describes himself as "avant-garde" is in danger of being merely gratuitous on the cultural scene, of being, to put it bluntly, a self-appointed snob.

RALPH: Of course, I am aware of the sort of vanguardist you have in mind. But he is an epigone, a usurper, a hanger-on. He is not the real thing. I admit that in the present state of cultural confusion it is as difficult to know a genuine avant-gardist when you see one as it is for the avant-gardist himself to recognize what his function is. But perhaps it will help if we consider the historical role of the avant-garde.

GEORGE: There have been sporadic vanguard movements at various places and times, but have they played a consistent part in the evolution of culture?

RALPH: Certainly. The avant-garde is the heir to the court circle of artists and intellectuals in Medieval and Renaissance times. With the breakdown of the aristocracy and the spread of literacy, the avant-garde assumed its historical role. After the eighteenth century, the democratization of culture and the new literacy confronted the advanced intelligence with a newly arisen welter of taste and opinion which, left to itself, found no other standards than the conformism, at once aggressive and complacent, of the bourgeoisie. In this situation the dissident intellectual, himself characteristically a bourgeois, found his mission. The mediocrity and, as it were, historical helplessness of his class in matters of art and ideas were an open invitation to his powers of discrimination and foresight. Thus, the avant-garde was brought into being *by the nature of bourgeois culture* (and later by that of socialist and communist culture); it is not historically gratuitous, as many people claim, and the familiar charge that by its very nature the vanguard perversely *alienates itself* from what is vaguely referred to as the broad healthy mainstream of culture will not stand up. Where would modern culture be without the great works which were in their day the product of avant-garde activity—*Lyrical Ballads, The Brothers Karamazov, Song of Myself, Mme. Bovary, Ulysses?* As Philip Rahv says, the avant-garde's "morality of opposition" has proved itself a success by the only test that counts, "the test of creative achievement." The vanguard might be said to begin with the French Encyclopedists, but a more distinctly modern form of cultural advance was to be seen in the German and English, and later in the French, romantic movements. The Wordsworth-Coleridge group was avant-garde in the modern sense, and in various countries and under varying conditions their kind of insurgence has been repeated in waves of forward-moving and receding energy.

GEORGE: But sometimes there is apparently no need for a vanguard. In the Victorian age not only the inferior writers but the truly great ones won more or less immediate public esteem and authority.

RALPH: True. But as usual in cultural matters the English analogy is misleading. In America the great writers, like Melville, Whitman, and James, were not the popular ones, and they had to content themselves with a fugitive notoriety and long neglect. In its contradictions and discontinuities American culture is like French and Russian culture rather than like the English. At certain periods of its history England has evolved an admirable middle culture, a main body of taste and opinion, into which the avant-garde, perhaps never radically alienated in the first place, could be temporarily absorbed, without detriment to the cul-

tural life of the nation. This has never happened in
America, where all the great things have been done by
lowbrows or by highbrows and where the middle culture, beginning with Howells, has been mediocre, has
too easily found its motives in commercialism and academic conformity, has incongruously patterned itself
on the English model, and has thus fundamentally mis-
understood and feared the really definitive characteristics of American culture.

GEORGE: I seem to scent a paradox. One thinks of
the avant-garde as perpetually rescuing mankind from
sterile traditions. Yet you speak of it as if it were a
tradition in itself.

RALPH: Yes, it has developed its own traditions.

GEORGE: Would you agree that because of its intransigent "morality of opposition" the vanguard is
even more subject to sterility and calcification than
other traditions?

RALPH: Yes. The necessary extremism of the avant-
garde, and its intensely articulated polemical attitude
not only give it dynamism but lay it open to rigidifica-
tion and sterility, whereas the very aimlessness of conventional culture saves it from these extremes.

To return to the current scene, let me propose to you
again that the avant-garde is not dead, but that its recent phase of "modernism" and experimentalism in the
arts is, after forty years of struggle and success, finally
exhausted. Why should it not be exhausted—consider-
ing that, as Joseph Frank says, we are now at the tail
end of "the greatest flowering of American arts and letters since New England Transcendentalism—a flowering that far surpasses the earlier one in force and orig-
inality." Without the concerted effort of the free spirits
of the time, in the flow and upsurge of their power,
this flowering would not have come about. We now inevitably find ourselves in a period of suspended anima-

tion and cultural confusion. If we are ever to set the ball rolling again, we have got to be clear first about the traditional significance of the avant-garde in its international and its native aspect and, second, about the cultural dialectic which in the past it has articulated and vivified in this country.

GEORGE: You think the insurgent movement which defended "modernism" in America—that is, the aesthetic experimentalism and social protest of the period between, say, 1912 and 1950—has expired of its own success?

RALPH: That is assuredly what has happened. Until recently the avant-garde writer, who made it his mission to promote "modernism," could feel that, in however limited a way, he was employed, so to speak, by history. Now he is more likely employed only by a university or a publishing house. The university and the publishing house have accepted Joyce, Pound, Eliot, Melville, James, Hemingway, and Faulkner—authors the avant-gardist once touted in vain—just as conclusively as Tennyson was ever accepted. And it appears that history no longer offers the insurgent intellectual or artist a job, or if it does, it is not the same job, and the particular tastes, ideas, and purposes it calls for are by no means clear.

GEORGE: I would like to hear what you have to say about that. But first, what evidence is there of a tradition of vanguard action in America? In the last century, I can think of only the Concord transcendentalists.

RALPH: That was the only successful avant-garde movement of the time. For the other writers of the last century it was mostly a matter of individual action. Whitman, in one sense a member of the transcendentalist group, was a kind of one-man vanguard with a number of sadly inferior disciples around him. We find two of the most isolated writers calling for what we should label a vanguard—Melville, with his plea for a "brotherhood" that will immediately proclaim the greatness of Hawthorne; Henry Adams, with his youthful plea to his brother that "what we want is a . . . school of our own generation."

But no such vanguard actually emerged until about 1912, when there appeared a genuinely concerted and insurgent intelligentsia, in dramatic response both to the historical demands and possibilities of American culture and in response to the international movement of "modernism." The tremendous energy liberated by this upsurge of creativity and criticism, despite the disasters that successively overtook it in the form of two World Wars and a great Depression, lasted for nearly forty years. There seems to be no generally accepted name for the six years or so after 1912 when the character of the modern movement in arts and letters was defined and the cultural energy we have been drawing on ever since was finally able to break through the conventional surface of American life. "Resurgence" is perhaps the most accurate word. The movement did not happen in a vacuum; it had been prepared (to look no farther back) by the social critics of the second half of the last century, notably Whitman, Adams, Howells, Bellamy, and Veblen. The ground had been laid, too, by the European heralds of modern times, such as Marx, Arnold, Shaw, Freud, and Nietzsche (whose writings constitute a magnificent philosophy and psychology of avant-garde action). It was the first time since the transcendentalist period that the barriers of provincialism were broken down and the most important minds of Europe were felt immediately, without being bowdlerized and filtered through the medium of genteel or middlebrow criticism.

GEORGE: This Resurgence would include, I suppose, the prophetic literary nationalism of Brooks and his associates, the poetic *risorgimento* of Ezra Pound and his group, the political-literary liberalism of Walter Lippmann and Herbert Croly in the *New Republic,* the pragmatism of Dewey, the New History of Beard and James Harvey Robinson, the popularized Nietzschean iconoclasm of Mencken, and so on.

RALPH: Correct. Powerful energies were liberated in that brilliant period. And despite the discontinuity of taste and opinion that characterized the three decades after 1920—so that a writer who felt culturally at home in 1920 felt totally at sea in 1930 and at sea all over again but in a different way in 1940—one could still draw on the emotional and intellectual capital of the Resurgence. This was true not only of the avant-garde but of the liberal middlebrow critics who soon began to oppose everything radical and extreme in modern culture, and it was true also of such momentary "counterrevolutionary" groups as the New Humanists.

Yet notwithstanding this continuity of energy in the midst of bewildering historical changes, there was a tragic wastefulness in the modern movement. The impact of the First World War fragmented and dispersed the Resurgence into the brilliant but unstable individual performances of the writers and artists of the 1920's. The economic pressures of the 1930's brought about a revival of the social concerns of 1912, but the generous and hopeful reform programs of the Resurgence were reduced to forms of doctrinaire politics, whether of the left or the right, which could not stand the test of time. The dispersal of energies in the 1920's and the reductive and repressive consolidations of the 1930's, historically inevitable as they may have been, left little cultural capital in the bank and failed to open up any significant new sources of renewal and recoupment.

The literary academicism of the 1940's was on the whole a fairly tame movement, although I cannot refrain from expressing my feeling that that period has been much maligned. The unintimidated critic is still wanting who will prove brave enough to defend a decade which saw the emergence of writers like Saul Bellow, Randall Jarrell, Robert Lowell, Ralph Ellison, Alfred Kazin, Isaac Rosenfeld, Mary McCarthy, and Leslie Fiedler among many others—a decade which, furthermore, if it was too academic, nevertheless came to understand American culture and its "usable past" much more accurately than they were ever understood before.

GEORGE: I see that is a subject close to your heart. I admire the writers you mention. At the same time I seem to find in your immediate contemporaries an intellectuality that is sometimes too savage, for my taste. They feel, perhaps too strongly, a need to assert themselves with an intense spirituality and wit; the *personae* they present to the world seem a bit too willed; they approach the surprised reader, as if bent on literary assault and battery. I suspect them of trying to convince themselves with various forms of emotional violence and fireworks that they are more than merely the last splutter and fizzle of a great creative era and I suspect some of them of pretending to a radical youth they never actually experienced. Their affinity with the potent revolutionaries of the first decades of the century is more than a little mythic. My own generation is not the first to live on borrowed experience— no offense, of course. But do go on. How does Van Wyck Brooks fit into the picture?

RALPH: You have certainly got a point about my contemporaries, and me. But to continue—in general one may say that all the clamoring spirits of 1912–18 were avant-garde, Brooks as much so as Ezra Pound.

After the war, however, a large segment left the avant-garde and, like Brooks himself, fell back on the cultural middle ground that had been prepared by Howells, the protean Howells, who had his complacent as well as his radical side. Brooks abdicated from modern culture about 1925, drawing back in horror from the genie whose bottle his early polemics had helped to unstopper. For behold! among the great writers who really spoke for the present and the future were Eliot, Joyce, Proust, Gide, Hemingway, and Pound, and they all seemed to Brooks culturally dangerous—they were, he said, undemocratic, highbrow, coterie writers.

Ever since Brooks' abdiction, one of the main debates of American intellectual life has been between the middlebrow and the highbrow (both claiming an affinity with or disowning the intellectually inarticulate lowbrow as it suited their purposes). The middlebrow claims to swim in the mainstream of life and of culture and accuses the highbrow of irrelevance, ignorance, and sterility. The highbrow retorts that the middlebrow's "mainstream of life and culture" is more than likely only the backwaters of history, or the stagnant waters of conventional success.

GEORGE: I remember only recently reading a blast at the avant-garde by Brooks in the *Times Book Review*. His manner was very Olympian; he called himself "we" and descended into the arena like Jove. He appeared to be under the impression that "avant-garde circles," as he called them, stretch from coast to coast, each submitting itself to the "party line." As far as I can see, that is the sheerest fantasy.

RALPH: Yes, I read the article. All that about a supposed "party line" is an example of the general tactic of those who say that the "critics" and the quarterly magazines now maintain a tight reactionary grip over the cultural life of America. The second step in this generally bogus argument is to present the reigning middlebrowism of our time as if it were a form of rebellion and fresh revolutionary activity instead of what it is—namely, the most successful form of cultural complacency in the Age of Eisenhower. Where and what is "the parent intellectual body" with which Brooks says the avant-garde should restore its ties? Where and what is "the mainland of American thinking" from which the "magic island" of the advanced intellectuals is detached? Not that these are necessarily meaningless concepts—but what *do* they mean?

GEORGE: Brooks' article would seem to be merely the latest expression of his lifelong search for the "focal center" of American culture. He still thinks of America, as you suggested yesterday, as if it were a nationalistic culture of the nineteenth-century sort.

RALPH: True. And I can only repeat that the concern of the critic nowadays should be exactly this alleged middle ground of culture, this more or less mythic center of taste and opinion—on the assumption, that is, that the duty of the critic is always to concern himself with whatever looks like the most powerful form of obscurantism and the most self-interested and successful kind of cultural mystique and polemic at any given time. There is no service in attacking the avant-garde critics, as everyone, including most of the critics themselves, is doing these days. It is all too clear what is wrong with them. Or if not, let me repeat: their specifically polemical task of the last forty years has expired with the success of the movements they championed. They have not yet clearly formulated what their duties in this interim period are. Meanwhile, they suffer from the well-known maladies of the avant-gardist, especially on the ebb tide of his influence: sterility, academicism, willful and excessive intellectuality.

GEORGE: You think, then, that the most forward-looking critics of the day should be trying to keep alive such imperfect dialectics as have been evolved in the effort to understand American culture, that they should be asking what is meant by "the parent intellectual body" and "the mainland of American thinking."

RALPH: Of course that is what they should be doing. But the familiar attitude is quite different. William Barrett expresses the widespread feeling of intellectuals when in a well-known essay, "Declining Fortunes of the Literary Review: 1945–57," he says, "since I have left the world of the highbrow, the terms 'highbrow' and 'lowbrow' do not seem to me to clarify human issues as much as I once thought they did." There is much to be said for this attitude, suggesting, as it does, two things—first, that the goal of the relaxed and enlightened man should be a flexibility of taste and, second, that the terms "highbrow" and "lowbrow" only imperfectly correspond to realities. But to this latter argument I am always moved to reply that (if I may repeat myself), imperfect as they are, they refer broadly to the main fact of our culture—its discontinuity and inner contradiction. These terms, or something like them, are therefore not dispensable, unless historically realistic statements about American culture are also dispensable.

Yet Barrett voices the tendency of the best critical minds of the time. For this is a time when the best critics try to achieve a flexible receptivity which allows them to be highbrow, lowbrow, middlebrow all at once, or if not all at once, then at appropriate moments. The best critics nowadays find an article like that of Brooks in the *Times*, or a highbrow reply to Brooks which uses the same terms, to be artificial. In other words, their ideal is to contain and express the contradictions of culture rather than to line up on one side or the other. Edmund Wilson, once a hero of radical intransigence, is now most admired for his flexibility and variousness.

GEORGE: What you just said reminds me of a passage in Lionel Trilling's essay on "Reality in America." Trilling is disputing Parrington's *Main Currents in American Thought* because Parrington pictured American culture as a flow of two currents, one of liberals and one of reactionaries—and I would suppose that Trilling's comments would apply as well to critics like the early Brooks, who thought of our culture as a flow of two currents, one of highbrows and one of lowbrows. Trilling says that culture is not a flow, but rather a struggle, a debate, in fact a dialectic. He goes on to say that there are likely to be certain artists in any culture who contain the dialectic within themselves, "their meaning and their power lying in their contradictions." He says that an unusually large number of the notable writers of the American nineteenth century were "repositories of the dialectic of their times," that they contained both the yes and the no of their culture, and that "by that token they were prophetic of the future." I gather that you agree with him on this.

RALPH: It is a simple but profound formulation. How indeed shall we understand Cooper, Melville, Hawthorne, Whitman, Faulkner and the rest unless we see how inexhaustibly they embody the contradictions of their culture? That we now understand them in this way is the surest sign of our general advance over the older simplifications and partialities of historical criticism. At the same time, Trilling's formulation may easily be made the banner of complacency. Look at what is at stake.

More and more critics and scholars of American literature are now taking a "dialectical" view of our literary history. They tell us that the American imagination from the beginning has embraced such contraries as Calvinism and secular optimism, romanticism and realism, and that it continues to do so. We thus have on our hands a disagreement between the new dialecticians and the old realists.

The old realists spoke of American writers and thinkers as being divided, not within themselves but *among* themselves, into Calvinists and secular progressives, romantics and realists, highbrows and lowbrows, or (in Philip Rahv's useful terms) palefaces and redskins. Much critical capital was made out of these broad distinctions, by applying the first terms of the above contrarieties to, say, Hawthorne, and the second to Whitman. To speak of Hawthorne, as many of the older writers did, as all moonbeams, cobwebs, and spiritual delicacy and of Whitman as the earthy realist and progressivist—this got one off toward a crude but undeniably instructive and necessary formulation of our cultural history. It became increasingly plain, however, particularly when the phenomenon of Melville began to loom clearly on the horizon, that many, and possibly most, of our most interesting writers have been like Melville in that they elude categories. Was Melville a paleface or a redskin? a Calvinist or a secular progressive? a romantic or a realist? a highbrow or a lowbrow? Clearly, as one goes down the list, the answer is always, "Both." Even Whitman, the alleged father of all realists and lowbrows or middlebrows, appears to have tipped us off correctly when he described himself as contradictory. Has anyone ever written a more refined and artificial poem than "When Lilacs Last in the Dooryard Bloom'd"?

GEORGE: But where is the danger? It seems to me that a real advance in accuracy has been made in perceiving that the characteristic contradictions of the

American imagination are to be thought of not so much as marking off from each other opposing camps of writers as forming, enlivening or, possibly, prostrating the minds of individual writers in all camps.

RALPH: Well, the danger in the dialectical view is this—that by sequestering cultural contradictions within the mind of this or that great author, we may be too easily led to the false conclusion that the contradictions no longer exist—that in, say, Melville or Whitman or Faulkner they are tamed and brought to rest, so that we don't need to worry about them any longer. But if we don't, we shall surely be different from these great authors themselves. Now, as for the "old realists"—and this is why I describe them with that phrase—their usual assumption was that Calvinism, romanticism, and gentility (if not highbrowism) were on the way out and that the history of modern American culture was the history of triumphant realism. In other words, this older account of our culture, as expressed, for instance, in Alfred Kazin's *On Native Grounds,* pictured our literary history as a more or less monolithic drive away from Puritan superstition, provincialism, gentility, and romanticism, and towards realism and naturalism in literature and a free, secular, and radically democratic culture.

Despite the large truth of the realists' view, it is clear that the progress of modern American literature is not monolithic. Gentility is always with us. As for Calvinism and romanticism, it is enough to observe that, without understanding and in some degree sympathizing with them, we can appreciate Dos Passos and Farrell but not Faulkner and Hemingway, Eliot, O'Neill, or Frost. Accordingly, the old animus against Puritanism and the romance element in American literature has had to be modified. They too are always with us.

Unhappily, the new dialecticians are mostly conservative and genteel by instinct. They are, to be sure, more subtle than the old realists, and in the details of literary analysis they are sometimes better critics. At the same time, their general view of things is conventional, their dialectic anything but intrepid. And contrasted with the vigorous, if often vague and rhetorical, spirit of the old radical realism, the cultural atmosphere the new dialecticians live in and in part create is more than a little stifling. For the too easy corollary to the new view is that since our great writers have from the beginning contained within themselves the contradictions of their culture, no fundamental change of taste and ideas has happened or can or should happen. The new dialecticians have lost sight entirely of the great, blunt truth which was all the old realists could see—namely, that despite every setback American literature *has* progressed since 1885 toward freedom, reality, and the assertion of radical democratic values. At the present moment, we need more than ever the insurgent spirit that was behind this advance, since the modern movement has temporarily lost its impetus.

GEORGE: You yourself have been presenting to me a dialectical view of American culture, and I am trying to disentangle you from what you call complacency and stifling conformity. I take it you mean that the real danger is not in a dialectical view but in a view that is not dialectical enough.

RALPH: Absolutely. Most of the critics of your generation who take any sort of position at all are dialectical only up to the point they want to get to—namely, some sort of middle ground of taste and opinion where contradictions are resolved, tensions relaxed, and the imagination moralized. There is among our younger critics a general drive to remove from art and from the psyche of the artist all conflict, recalcitrancy, suffering, and neurosis, all color, native impulse, and adventure.

And thus, so far as all this affects American studies, an anomalous situation has developed. For the most general truth about the reigning fashions of criticism is that they aim at a middle ground where contradictions are resolved, whereas the most general truth about American literature is that at its best it has been remarkable for its unique capacity to express the extreme and irreconcilable aspects of life and for its habit of leaving ultimate questions open.

GEORGE: I would think that you have found a disturbing anomaly there. But by its very nature criticism has to have assumptions that differ from those of what is criticized. Also, one of the functions of criticism is adjudication, a careful weighing of issues, an attempt at equable judgment. In this sense at least it seems by nature to search for a middle ground.

RALPH: Oh, I don't imply that criticism should share the assumptions of what it criticizes—merely that it should be *aware* of what it criticizes, and aware of it as something that may be incongruous with the projected desires of the critic.

But to get back to the avant-garde—what has happened to it in our versatile culture of the 1950's is a psychological equivalent of what has happened to it sociologically. Sociologically, it has been institutionalized by the universities and the publishers, which by definition means that in its modern phase it has come to an end. At the same time, it has been internalized, so to speak, in the flexibly dialectical mind of contemporary criticism. In this temporary withdrawal from the field of action it finds a possibility of continued life. The resiliency of the best critical minds must be counted on to keep the avant-garde attitude alive during periods which have no immediate task for its polemical mission.

Yet the task of the temperamental or born avant-garde critic is not limited to converting the philistines to art. He is also perennially the disinterested student and historian of culture, looking into the past and the present for the radical and not merely the contingent and incidental facts. The past convinces him that discontinuity and contradiction have always been of the essence of American culture. The present convinces him that among critics only the most powerful and resilient of "versatile" minds are capable of keeping alive the avant-garde spirit, or any spirit, or of embodying cultural contradictions of any sort without collapsing under the great strain into a formless middle way of feeling and thought. Who can doubt that this formless middle way of feeling and thought, with its moralism and conventionality, has hardened into the new "cake of custom"? As for the future, one can only believe that the end of the present interim period will be marked by a new resurgence from the uneasy subliminal depths of our culture, in the classic manner of avant-garde action—provided, that is, that 1950 marks the end of a phase of American culture as we have known it, and not the end of that culture itself.

GEORGE: Ah, that is the thought that keeps coming into my head, because I too see a distinct possibility of a basic change in American culture. I cannot help feeling that your view of the American future contains only two alternatives: either American culture will continue to be what it has always been, only on a bigger scale, or, it will be a vast desert of suburban conformity, an immensely overpopulated hive of mindless drones, who will not even know what the word "culture" means. I think your first alternative is closer to the truth but that nevertheless a real change, for which you are not prepared, is taking place. Therefore, if you don't mind my saying so, I think that the kind of cultural critique which you derive from writers like Tocqueville, Whitman, Emerson, Henry Adams, and the early Brooks, is already beginning to be archaic. Brilliant as it is, and true as it is, it is already being outmoded by history. Think for example, how unlikely it is that there will ever be any more writers like Faulkner and Hemingway—they belong to an older America, in which the frontier and the forest were still at the forefront of the imagination, where the stresses and strains of Calvinism were present, and where there was distinct regional feeling. To use David Riesman's handy terms, your critique belongs in essence to the older, Calvinist, production-oriented, inner-directed America.

Now as for your second alternative—a total, or, as it were, totalitarian conformity without any culture except that of the mass media or at best a feeble middlebrowism—I agree that this is a danger. But I rest my hope on an ever-growing cultivated minority. To you they will seem "middlebrow." But you must admit that there are real middlebrow virtues—those first articulated and defended by Howells. Middlebrowism itself is becoming steadily more flexible, humane, and serious. It is no longer automatically a form of mediocrity or Babbittry. Enlightened publishers and professors have grown more and more hospitable to talents of a high order—of the sort which formerly in this country they would take seriously only after a long avantgarde campaign. For example, Dylan Thomas quickly gained such popularity as comes to difficult poets without much intervention of avant-garde critics. The paperback classics, old and new, have discovered a fairly large audience of discerning readers. You have made me newly aware of how the middle culture resists definition and of how it is easily used as a mask for mere complacency and hatred of intellect and art. Yet the statistics show a fairly widespread patronage of serious art, music, architecture, and writing the country over by people who are not in any sense avant-gardists.

From what you have been saying about the necessity of historical realism in cultural discussion, I know that you must be theoretically prepared for the possibility of definitive historical change. One must roll with the punch of history. From your own admission of a feeling that real changes in the quality of American culture may be happening, I make bold to proclaim dogmatically that they are. I am quite happy to admit that I don't know exactly *what* they are and to rely on a basic animal optimism which suggests to me that things won't turn out too badly. Thus, my dear Ralph, I take my mild revenge for your not too successfully hidden idea that I am a middling, unimaginative sort of fellow—a Sancho Panza in fact—by suggesting with all due respect to a friend and a host that when you talk about radicalism and the avant-garde, there is about you more than a touch of Don Quixote.

RALPH: I don't presume to do so, but I would rather remind you of Whitman and Melville and Mark Twain, of Veblen and Dreiser and Darrow, of John Jay Chapman and Edmund Wilson and Van Wyck Brooks.

Sunday Evening:

Past and Future

George, Ralph, and Rinaldo, at Crane's Beach, sit atop a sand dune in the tough grass whose roots keep the dune from being gradually blown away by the weather. But there is no wind tonight. Below, on the beach, Nancy, Dorothy, and the children are resting, after the swim, the baseball game, and the picnic supper. As the sun sets behind the dunes, the quiet sea takes on a variety of pink and violet colors. Beyond the mile-long sand bar, now above water as the tide recedes, is a long strip of slick silvery water through which a yawl with its sails furled makes its silent way. The first lights at Newburyport can be seen on the coast to the north. The whole scene is suffused with austere and delicate light and a perfect calm prevails.

RINALDO: Lucky Americans! To have beaches like this, with miles and miles of fine white sand. There is nothing like it anywhere in the Old World.

RALPH: For the preservation of the beach and the adjacent acres of marsh and upland we have the great American phenomenon of plumbing to thank. It was once the estate of the Crane family, magnates of the cloaca. They turned it all over to a commission of philanthropic private citizens who maintain it for the benefit of the public. The massive and well-plumbed *palazzo*, on the hill there, has real imported Italian gardens. Cultural events take place there during the summer, and the vacationing squirearchy of the North

Shore shows up in large numbers to attend the concerts and dance recitals. They seem very eager for culture in pleasant surroundings, although a good many of them are obviously so full of lobster and gin that they seem to be conscious only of their own drugged fatuity. Bob Adamant reports that often in winter you can see white-tailed deer hereabouts, foraging in the snow for beach grass, cranberry leaves, and birch shoots. One can feel here that America is not yet spoiled, not yet totally populated and paved or, as the real estate dealers say, "improved" from coast to coast. There is still time to feel the unpopular emotion of piety and thankfulness for the gift of this magnificent New World, despite the fact that the two patrolmen in the jeep will not allow us to forget for long the always present Bureaucratic Big Brother.

GEORGE: Oh, they're just a couple of college boys, trying to get along.

RINALDO: I sometimes think, Professor, that you would have been happier in the forests with Natty Bumppo than you are in modern America.

RALPH: Well, that is merely a romantic self-indulgence. Actually there have been many moments in our history when I should like to have been around—moments of cultural awakening. I would like to have been a young man in 1776, 1830, or 1912. As it is, I am grateful to have had the experience of being young during the days of FDR and the New Deal. Since then the spiritual deadlock of the cold-war period has been broken at best by only one or two inspiring events— a minor one, the election of Truman in 1948, and a major one, the Hungarian revolution.

RINALDO: And do you see nothing in the future?

RALPH: As usual when I am talking with you I seem to see into the future. I see in the deepening color of the eastern horizon the promise of a new dawn. I can imagine that the driftwood fire Darlene and her brother are lighting for the children is the beacon of a new America in the days to come. Meanwhile, I suggest that to conclude the conversation of the week end we attempt a bit of recapitulation and prophecy. May I ask you, George, what political future you see for America?

GEORGE: It will be what we have now, basically. A liberal, socially responsible capitalism with about the same New Deal content it has had under Eisenhower.

RALPH: And abroad?

GEORGE: The gradual defeat of imperialist Communism by economic competition, diplomatic persuasion, and technical superiority in peace and war.

RALPH: And Rinaldo?

RINALDO: At home I see a capitalism steadily modified in the direction of democratic socialism. I see more decentralization, more local autonomy, a new respect for the individual. Abroad, I see the final defeat of Communism as the result of political and ideological superiority. We must stop giving the peoples of the world nothing but arms and machines. We must help them to self-determination and a better way of life. The world needs freedom and a humane, creative politics, not moral hypocrisy, threats, gadgets, and Madison Avenue copy writers.

Above all, I fear there may be an incalculably dangerous complacency in George's words about our "technical superiority." Undoubtedly we have it in many areas, but probably not in others. We make a thousand times more automobiles, TV sets, and other comforts and conveniences than the Russians do. But do you know for a fact, George, that we are ahead of the Russians in all technological fields?

GEORGE: No, I confess I don't. I had only assumed. . . .

RINALDO: I doubt if we can afford to "assume." Since I have impressed you with my general optimism, let me qualify by saying that I have sometimes felt the hand of death at the throat of our America. I will give you one small and apparently inconsequential instance which I happened to encounter the other day. *The National Geographic Magazine* has recently published a history of itself. It indulged in much self-congratulation because over the years the magazine had transformed itself "from one of cold scientific fact into a vehicle for carrying the living, breathing, human-interest truth about the world." Now, science is of course a cold intellectual discipline, or it is not science. And to saturate, blur, and obliterate its intellectual quality with purely emotional, sociological, psychiatric, and commodity values, which is what in effect the *Geographic* prides itself on having done, is to instigate a possibly disastrous breakdown of intellect and will, however good it may be for circulation figures. Not that the *Geographic* was ever, as far as I know, an important scientific journal. I merely cite it as unfortunately illustrative of the state of mind of the vast majority of our compatriots.

GEORGE: I can agree with at least some of what you say. But I've grown cynical about world affairs. It seems to me the most a fellow can do nowadays is cultivate his garden, like Candide.

RINALDO: But when you look up from the rows of beets and cabbages——

GEORGE: Okra and rosemary——

RINALDO: And survey the world and the place of the United States in it, I should think you would be conscious of a frightening feeling of drift. Eisenhower's administration is full of moralistic talk, but it is mindless and fatalistic. There is no hand on the tiller and the passengers on the ship of state can only hope for the best. Excuse me for metaphorically mixing up gardens and ships.

RALPH: You are still bent on being an engineer? I think you would be more valuable as a pamphleteer, an editor, or a Congressman.

RINALDO: I don't rule out any of those possibilities. You American intellectuals are always forgetting that this is still the land of promises and opportunities. I like engineering because it gets me in touch with America and its capacity to move, change, remake, and build things. I hope to go in for civil engineering and have a chance to work on some great bridge, dam, highway or military installation. I shall not be disfiguring America; rather I shall be learning what is entailed in the great problem of conservation. I shall really know what is involved when I enter the fight against the misuse of natural resources by private power combines and the business oligarchs.

GEORGE: Would you work for one of the great corporations?

RINALDO: Certainly. I want to make a little money, for one thing. Besides, I admire and like American businessmen. They have imagination and force of character, although they do not yet know how to use these qualities in a statesmanlike manner. I do not wish to destroy them but only to lead them to see where in the long run their own best self-interest lies. Europeans are often ghost-ridden by history, but the notorious failing of Americans is the short view they take. Like the intellectuals during the last decade, the businessmen are fatalists. Thus they tend to fall back on greed, the impulse of the moment, and an attitude of *après moi le déluge*. They will see finally the advantage of long-range planning, of conservation, of decentralization, and of economizing, of cutting down on the mad overinflation of advertizing costs.

GEORGE: And the labor unions?

RINALDO: Some of them have shown genuine states-manship. Yet they tend to model themselves too much on big business and big government, competing for in-fluence and the fruits of a rich economy on the same grounds and with no clearer moral principles or ends in view than the others.

RALPH: You must find American engineers a pretty stuffy and ignorant lot. What do they think of you? Do they call you a Red?

RINALDO: Oh, they're not so bad. Of course they are not so politically alert or so cultivated as European en-gineers. Almost any engineer in Europe knows some-thing not only about his own literature but about American literature too. I doubt if many American en-gineers have even heard of Melville or Thoreau or Veblen or William James, except maybe on a quiz pro-gram. As for my political opinions, I've never made a secret of them and have never had any trouble. I've worked for the Acme Construction Company for two summers now and they have offered me a good job after I graduate from engineering school. They seem prepared to accept some odd opinions from a citizen who was until recently a European and who still speaks with an accent. As for the future, I don't want to argue with them—merely to impress upon them with facts and figures and pragmatic results the direction in which their best future lies. They don't respect dialec-tic and argumentation, but I believe they are getting ready to respect history. When they are able to do that, America will be a better civilization. It will be on firmer grounds, and the ghost of Henry Ford, who said that "history is bunk," will be laid forever. The Depres-sion was the first great shock in this process. You don't find the younger businessmen and engineers blaming all the troubles of their class on bad luck or on a fatalistic idea of boom-and-bust capitalism. They don't go along, either, with the villain theory of history that their fathers believed in, casting FDR, of course, in the role of Satan. They begin at last to see America as an evolving economy with a past and a future, not as a capitalistic Garden of Eden from which Satan must be tossed out. They see now that neither the Garden of Eden nor anything else exists outside of time and change. The intellectuals have been telling them this for generations, but the businessmen have had to learn it in their own way. However, the old fatalism and short-run opportunism still beckon, particularly when they are swathed in the plausible rhetoric of Eisenhower's "modern Republicanism."

RALPH: I can see that you have studied up on America.

RINALDO: Before I was twenty and while I was still in Europe I had read with amazement many of your great authors. One of the first things I discovered when I got to America in 1950 was that I was more interested in America than the Americans were. Also I have had excellent tutors, in yourself and in our friend George here, with whom I used to talk in college. I am still interested in America. The vast distances! The magnificent superhighways—one can drive from New York to Chicago almost without seeing a traffic light; one sees hundreds and hundreds of miles of forest and open farm land.

RALPH: You drive on the thruways in a 1951 Chevrolet?

RINALDO: It has a 1955 V-8 engine, of which I have taken excellent care. It has carried me from coast to coast. My American friends told me that the midwest cities were boring because they were all the same. But I will never forget the thrill of seeing Omaha and Cleveland and Indianapolis rising up out of the plain.

I admit that when you get into these cities you find slums and rampant, exploitative housing and commercial developments along with much gaudy wealth. But this does not spoil things for me. It gives me a challenge. The cities and Levittowns are still new—spiritually new, I mean. They are not sunk in the centuries-old weariness and despair of European cities. They can still be changed.

GEORGE: You are not shocked by our countrymen's lack of culture and by their social conformity?

RINALDO: Oh, as for culture, you either have it or you haven't. Americans worry too much about culture; you can't worry it into being. As for conformity, I am so busy trying to bring nonconformity back into American life that I don't have time to be shocked.

RALPH: Yet surely your high hopes for America must have left you open to disillusionment, when you got to know the country firsthand?

RINALDO: Yes, yes, that is true. From my reading and from the legend of the America of the past I had expected to find a nation electric with political activity. What else was one to expect in the country of Jefferson and Madison, of Lincoln and Douglas, of La Follette and Bryan, of Norris and the Roosevelts? I envisioned in America hundreds of politically alert local newspapers and radio stations; I imagined the vital ideas of democracy being perpetually discussed on the hustings at every rural crossroad and in every town hall. I even supposed that the relatively well-to-do youth who go to colleges and universities would express political ideas.

But what did I find? A local population everywhere in the country who seem to have surrendered political decisions either to the federal government or to the lottery of contending pressure groups—to the mere free-for-all, that is, of organized piracy in which the bankers, the loan sharks, the real estate operators, the private power companies, the communications interests, the cynical and irresponsible "services," the labor unions, the corporations and combines, all scramble for the spoils. The average citizen seems to respond to this spectacle of rapine and chaos not with a creative politics but only with cynicism and apathy. Yet the statistics show that rich as are the natural and human resources of America, they are not inexhaustible. America can be despoiled. I confess it is disheartening sometimes to think that whereas the history of Europe has been the long chronicle of the plunder of one nation by another, America seems bent on becoming the first nation that ever plundered itself.

GEORGE: You were surprised at the surrender of local autonomy?

RINALDO: Yes. I imagined that in a democracy of enlightened citizens the most liberal parts of government would be those closest to the people—the town councils, the state legislatures, the House of Representatives. I was dismayed to find that Americans look only to the highest officers of the land—the President and the Supreme Court—to defend the heritage of democratic rights and principles, and that all the lower branches of government are assumed to be irresponsible, reactionary, or ignorant.

RALPH: That's really a dangerous situation.

RINALDO: It certainly is. For one thing, in a democracy the surrendering of moral responsibility to an elite generates a hatred and suspicion of that elite. Its members are suspect on two grounds—because they are by the nature of their office paternal and aristocratic, and because they speak in the language of the Constitution, especially the Bill of Rights, and thus incur the suspicion of being dangerous radicals. What happens, then, if the shaky national grip on its democratic principles is relaxed entirely and both the Presidency and the Court are staffed with people who have no more knowledge of and devotion to American democracy than Congressman Hodgepodge of Ohio?

RALPH: It is clear that a general reconstruction of politics is necessary, beginning at the local level. But is there any material left to work with? I mean, have you found any substance in the Russian charges that the American populace is drugged by the opiates of mass entertainment, alcohol, popular psychiatry, and tranquilizers?

RINALDO: No, no. Americans are restless. They feel guilt. They are worried about their children and the future. Almost any American, if you appealed to his better side, would admit the truth of what we have just been saying. I believe they can be counted on to recapture the local self-determination they have lost.

RALPH: The tone of the times has been created by the suburban new-rich. They are the new barbarians in our midst—the people whose rear fender fins are longer and higher than anyone else's, the people who decorate their ranch houses with neon lights at Christmas time and whose idea of aesthetic propriety is the juke box. They are the characters who don't mind spending a thousand dollars for a freezer or five thousand for a swimming pool or laying out the money for car number two or television set number three so long as they don't have to spend anything to raise the salaries of the public school teachers—the teachers whom they count on to keep their children from becoming juvenile delinquents and whom they accuse of being Communists if, as often happens, their children *become* juvenile delinquents.

GEORGE: Yes, it is always the *arriviste* who is dangerous and needs to be educated. In any American community the ordinary people and the older well-to-do families are more responsible.

RALPH: But just at the moment there seem to be so many new-rich that they are not so much a minority problem as a mass movement.

RINALDO: I don't think the statistics would bear that out. Most of the sociologists you literary people as well as the general public have been reading have made their studies in the new suburbs around New York and Chicago. If you look at the country as a whole you will find relatively few swimming pools, but you will find, as always, much plain living and much actual hardship.

RALPH: You say you were surprised to find so little political awareness in the colleges and universities?

RINALDO: Yes, I was. And I was saddened all over again during the Hungarian revolution. For the students in Budapest, and also in East Germany, in Poland, in Spain, perhaps in Russia itself, the possibility of a radical politics and a humane culture suddenly came into being. The best aspirations of youth had become a matter of daily life and death, until they were snuffed out by a brutal repression which America was either powerless or unwilling to oppose. I fear many Americans regarded the Hungarian revolution as merely one more event that turned up between the commercials on the TV screen. As for the American students, they continued, with a few exceptions, to be "cool"—that being their taste not only in jazz but in politics, ideas, dress, sex, and literature. If you will forgive me, George, I seem to see in you a tendency to be cool on certain occasions when heat or cold might be more appropriate.

GEORGE: I imagine you are right. To be frank, I am not entirely happy about it. But are you going to exonerate Ralph?

RINALDO: Not quite. He is not "cool," but I think he is a bit alienated from reality. He sometimes reminds me of those politically minded professors whose politics is partly a nostalgia for their own youth. In the long lists of Intellectuals for Stevenson that appeared in the papers—the New York papers, that is—in 1952 there seemed to be many professors, writers, publishers, actors, and scientists, who were under the illusion that they were supporting a new FDR, who would take to Washington with him a new generation of Leon Hendersons, Harold Ickeses, and Adolph Berles. I doubt if many of them took a real look at the new post-war America. If they had, they would have been less enthusiastic about Stevenson, in spite of his graceful syntax—I do not deny that in many ways he is an admirable man.

RALPH: Yes, you are right about that. I count on you, our new Tocqueville, to report to us the findings of a fresh and objective view.

RINALDO: I don't believe I am a new Tocqueville, but if I am, I can assure you that I will not, like my predecessor, return to Europe a convinced conservative; rather I shall stay here and help to reconstruct a radical democracy in America.

RALPH: I propose now that before we join the others around the fire we each try to express the ideal value—from the cultural point of view—of the life we have been leading and of the thinking we have done. As the oldest, I shall begin—quite unencumbered by modesty. I have tried to give new striking power to the tradition of radical criticism in this country—the tradition that includes Emerson, Whitman, Henry Adams, Veblen, the early Van Wyck Brooks, and others. In order to keep up a steady dissent from the conformism and middlebrowism of the time, I have shown how little these are justified by the best traditions of

American culture and American literature. In the face
of an interim culture which seems bent on closing out
the possibility of conflict, diversity, and intellectual
struggle, I have tried to give new intelligibility, relevance, and concreteness to such cultural dialectics as
have been arrived at by the best observers of the
American scene. I have tried to show that American
literature and the native habits of mind it reflects provide little or no basis for a conservative view of things
but that they provide a tradition of radical criticism
and democratic affirmation. I have sought out the
grounds on which a cultural radicalism and humane
avant-garde may be said to be alive at present and to
imagine how they may assert greater influence in the
future. In varying terms, some of them happily chosen,
others not, this has been the arduous and sustained
task of what will doubtless turn out to have been the
most intellectually active decade of my life.

GEORGE: The effort of my life so far has been less
ideological and far-reaching. My generation learned,
perhaps too well, to distrust ideas such as those to
which Ralph clings. We decided for ourselves, or were
told, that they did not work, that the test had been
made in the radical decades of the 1920's and 1930's,
and that the leading ideas of the time had proved to
be too abstract, too ambitious, and too crude. We gath-
ered also that the older ideas resembled the credos of
the totalitarian movements, and we felt that unless we
were liberals of a very conservative and disillusioned
kind, we were in danger of being Stalinists. We found
our elders to be ignorant of the facts of life. We became realists. This meant that we accepted *realpolitik*
and stalemate on the national and international scene.
But we found a justification for this cynicism (if that
is what it was) in our discovery of the ordinary life.
In this sense our new realism has turned out to be valu-

able. For we live more comfortably than our elders in the actual conditions of life. We are more at peace with our own emotions; we know and understand and like people; we are wise in the ways of sex, of family life, of community activity. We know intimately and exactly the page-by-page texture of literature and, as it were, of life. We know our children; they are not, as perhaps they were for some of our elders, mere ciphers or annoyances. In conclusion, we made the best of the cold-war situation—by converting a culpable but, as it seemed, inescapable *realpolitik* into a saving and illuminating and much-needed realism of the immediate moral life. We can claim to have become experts in those activities which are most intimate, most continuous, most unavoidable, and, thus, most human. Ours is the wisdom of the ordinary.

RINALDO: Excellent. In these two graphic self-portraits I already see myself. I realize that in order to simplify, you have both somewhat caricatured yourselves. I shall do likewise. Ideally, I should like to be the synthesis suggested by Ralph's thesis and George's antithesis. My ideal is to give concrete relevance and dynamic realization to Ralph's criticism of culture, and to give intellectual and moral significance, as well as energy and daring, to George's commonsensical and intuited realism. Time will tell how I, and all of us, make out.

RALPH: In history everything capable of clarity is made clear. Meanwhile, let us congratulate ourselves on having listened to each other. Patiently listening to each other is something that during these interim years people have not been doing, especially intellectuals. And now the children are singing. Let us join the rising republic around the fire.

Date Due

JAN 25 '67			
⑬	PRINTED	IN U. S. A.	